UNDERSTANDING SOCCER

Rules & Procedures For Players, Parents & Coaches

GENE KIRA

APPLES & ORANGES, INC.

VALLEY CENTER, CALIFORNIA

ISBN 0-929637-02-X
First Printing 1994

Library of Congress Cataloging-in-Publication Data:

Kira, Gene, 1946-
        Understanding soccer : rules & procedures for players, parents & coaches / by Gene Kira.
            p.   cm.
        Includes index.
        ISBN 0-929637-02-X : $9.95
        1. Soccer--Rules--Juvenile literature.   I. Title
GV943.4.K57   1993
796.334'02'022--dc20   93-20748
                                                                              CIP
                                                                              AC

Printed in the United States of America
Published by Apples & Oranges, Inc., P.O. Box 2296, Valley Center, CA 92082
Telephone: 619-751-8868   Fax: 619-751-8866

Dedicated to all the Loose Cannons and Killer Bees of the world...
May each of you, in your own way, someday score that big goal!

Acknowledgements

Of the many people who contributed to the creation of this book, I am particularly indebted to the following:

Javier Aviles; Linda, Gregor and Zackery Bonin; Mario Cozzi and the Valley Center Hurricanes; Alex and Christine Gifford; Oscar Haros; John Hoogenboom; Ruth Hoogenboom; John Johnstone, Glasgow/Encinitas; Gifford and Abigail Kira; Nicole Morcombe; Kevin Murphy; John Napier of John Napier Soccer Camps; Lee Popejoy; Craig Studenka; Joel Velazquez; Micah Walker. — gsk

CONTENTS

"...Every Loose Cannon gave chase, even their goalie..."

If <u>You</u> Didn't Grow Up With Soccer...

Late summer had turned to early fall, and the Loose Cannons hadn't won a game.

Every Saturday, they had come, parents and siblings trailing behind them with folding chairs and ice chests full of Gatorade and orange slices, all elbows and knees, and in the sun they looked like wind-blown confetti, as they hopped and fell and swirled up and down the field.

They ran until it seemed they would burst, and after each defeat, they gathered about their coach for another round of "Two, four, six, eight... Who do we appreciate?"

The first game against the Killer Bees had probably been the low point of the season, not so much because of the 6-0 loss, but because it was then that the Loose Cannons had secretly stopped believing they could win. Ever since that game, there had been a lot more standing around, a certain thinness to the cheering on the sidelines, and a few missing hands when it was time to "Two, four, six, eight..."

And, ever since that game, there had seemed to be less indignant confusion among the parents when a foul was called, or the referee blew his whistle for the mysterious "offside" violation.

Yet... yet... the Cannons still showed up every Saturday, and now it had come down to the final half of the final game of the year, and the Killer Bees were faltering. With only a few minutes remaining, the scored stood tied, amazingly, at 0–0.

Perhaps because they had already given up hope, the Cannons had hung back defensively for the entire game, and no amount of furious swarming and stinging by the Bees had been able to break through their indifferent but impenetrable formation.

The Bees huffed and puffed and attacked again and again, but every shot ricocheted off the Cannons' legs as though trapped in a pinball machine.

Slowly, so slowly the tide was turning in the Cannons' favor as the Killer Bees ran themselves out of gas.

Now, a sudden clearing kick sent the ball toward the Bees' goal, and every Loose Cannon gave chase, even their goalie. The parents all stood, as the Cannons left the bigger, faster, but somnolent Bees far behind and entered unfamiliar territory.

A shot! Another shot! The Bees' goalie lay flat on his stomach, and watched helplessly as the ball bounced off the back of a Loose Cannon, and wandered through the corner of the goal, coming to rest against the back side of a goal-post.

A win! The Cannons hollered and leapt into each other's arms, and high-stepped in aimless circles with their hands held high and their fingers pointing skyward. Where did they learn to do *that*?

As their parents and coaches watched in stunned disbelief, the Cannons gathered themselves together for one last "Two, four, six, eight...", and then lined themselves up, unaided, on the halfway-line to shake hands with the defeated Killer Bees.

Then, they came running off their field of victory, giving high-fives all around, rummaging through the ice chests for their orange slices and cookies.

Just kids again, until next season.

* * *

Soccer is a wonderful sport, especially for young children, who seem to grasp the basics of the game from the moment they step on the field.

For many Americans, though, soccer is a relatively new and mysterious pastime. It is a credit to soccer's amazing virtues as a sport, that we can enjoy it so much, while understanding so little about it!

The purpose of *Understanding Soccer* is to explain the game in a clear, easy-to-understand way for players, parents, coaches, grandparents, and fans of all ages.

Understanding Soccer is an easy-to-read, yet comprehensive explanation of both the official rules and the unwritten traditions of this exciting sport.

Newcomers to soccer will be able to play it correctly or enjoy it as spectators after a single, relatively painless reading of this book.

Some Basic Concepts

Soccer is a ball-kicking game in which two teams play each other on a rectangular field about the size and shape of an American football field.

The ball is somewhat smaller than a basketball.

Each team defends an upright, rectangular goal at its end of the field, and the object of the game is to kick the ball through the other team's goal as many times as possible.

FIFA: The Official Rules

The official rules of soccer are contained in a deceptively thin little booklet called the *Laws of the Game* which is published each year by the international governing body, FIFA (fee'-fah). There are 17 "Laws" covering various aspects of soccer matches.

FIFA, established in 1904, stands for the Fédération Internationale de Football Association, which is located in Zurich, Switzerland. FIFA sets the rules, authorizes referees, and sanctions competition around the world.

FIFA has authorized the United States Soccer Federation (USSF) to administer the sport in the United States. Most U.S. youth leagues, adult leagues, school leagues and professional leagues play under guidelines established by the USSF.

Many school leagues and youth leagues play under rules slightly different from the official FIFA *Laws of the Game*. These rule modifications often involve the duration of the games, the size of the balls, and other accommodations for young players.

Official FIFA, college, and youth rule books may be obtained from the addresses listed in the "Resources" section on page 78.

The Real World — Soccer Variations

While a few referees might argue that the *Laws of the Game* are applied with perfect coherence, this is not the case.

Quite apart from the known, codified rule adaptations that have been created for indoor soccer and youth soccer, there exist individual and regional variations on how the official rules are interpreted. No two referees will call a match in *exactly* the same way, and it is part of the inherent charm and appeal of soccer that these variations exist.

The reader may take comfort in the knowledge that variations in how the rules are applied are usually minor, and are usually a matter of degree, *e.g.*, referees might disagree on the exact amount of protection from body contact a goal-keeper is entitled to while playing in the penalty-area.

The rules and procedures presented in this book are the "standard" ones used during outdoor, adult soccer games. Whatever the match, however, the information presented here will allow the spectator or player to enjoy the game and understand it.

What's "Fair-Charging"?

Officially, the only body contact allowed in soccer is a stylized form of gentlemanly, shoulder-to-shoulder bumping called "charging," "shoulder-charging," or "fair-charging." Fair-charging, theoretically, is permitted only with the arms down and the body erect. The bumping action is supposed to be non-violent, confined to the *sides* of the shoulders, and incidental to legitimate efforts to play the ball. Charging against the chest area, or against the fronts and backs of the shoulders is technically illegal, as is charging against the spine.

In actual practice, soccer is a fairly rough contact sport, with collisions and body entanglements of all sorts occurring constantly. When these collisions are blatantly intentional and have nothing to do with playing the ball, they are penalized as fouls. However, the vast majority of body contacts are considered to be accidental, and thus part of normal play.

Violent or dangerous charging—especially from behind or with a swing of the arm—is penalized. However, even very "vigorous" charging is allowable as long as it is "fair," *i.e.*, shoulder-to-shoulder while playing the ball.

Fair-charging, shoulder-to-shoulder.

You "Tackle" The Ball, Not The Player

As opposed to American football, a "tackle" in soccer does *not* refer to wrestling an opponent to the ground. In soccer, to "tackle" means to block the ball with the feet in a way that causes an opponent to lose control of it. The intention must be to play the ball, not the opponent. Incidental contact with the opponent is allowed, but only during a legitimate play for the ball, and generally, only after contacting the ball, or simultaneously with contacting the ball.

As in charging, legal tackling in soccer can be so "vigorous" that the victim is indeed knocked to the ground. Generally, this happens after contact with the ball has been made, and either the tackler's foot or the ball itself bumps the opponent's feet.

However, the main intent must always be to play the ball, not the opponent.

Tackling from behind, especially, must be done skillfully and without tripping, or a foul will be called. Some referees may penalize virtually any attempt to tackle from behind.

A soccer tackle is intended to capture the ball, not wrestle an opponent to the ground.

Notes On The Text

• In the interest of brevity and clarity, the male pronoun "he" has been used when referring to players, coaches and referees, rather than the more correct "he or she." Be assured, though, that when we say "he," what we *really* mean is "he or <u>she</u>"!

• Other conventions used throughout the text include using the word "kick" to mean contacting the ball with any legal part of the body. In most cases, this includes any part of the body except the hands and arms. Thus, when we describe the ball as being "kicked" through a goal, it usually also means knocking or driving it through the goal with the head, chest, thighs — or any other part of the body except the hands and arms. Exceptions to this usage are noted in the text.

• The term "kick-off" has been used to refer to the initial kick taken to begin play at the beginning of the game, after a goal has been scored, after halftime, and to begin overtime periods. The kicks themselves are more properly referred to as "place-kicks," with the term "kick-off" reserved for the *taking* of the kick. To keep things simple, "kick-off" here refers to any kick, or the taking of any kick to begin play or restart play from the center-mark.

• The term "goal-keeper" has been used rather than "goalie," which is actually more popular among younger players. "Goal-keeper" or just "keeper" is the more traditional usage at the adult level.

• The term "kicking-to-the-keeper" describes the recently prohibited maneuver of kicking the ball into the hands of one's own goal-keeper.

• The term "pseudo-minor-foul" has been coined to encompass a group of technical violations that are described piecemeal in the official rules, yet are all treated in a similar fashion, *i.e.*, as minor-fouls.

• There is a fair amount of repetition of the material presented from one section to another. This slows the reading somewhat, but it has been done in the interest of clarity, and in order to allow each section to stand on its own.

• Although the meanings of all soccer terms used here are either explained on first usage, or may be inferred from context, the reader may find it useful to take an early look through the glossary that begins on page 68.

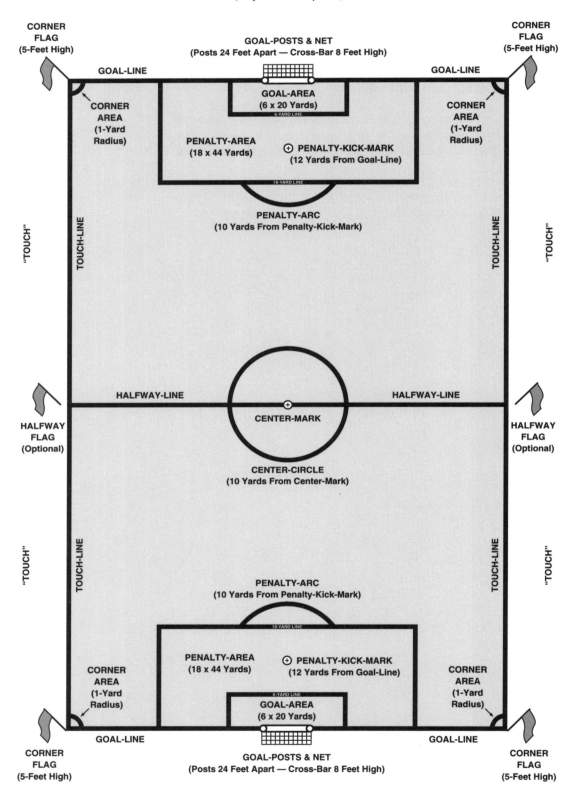

Length = 100-130 Yards
Width = 50-100 Yards

(May not be a square.)

CORNER FLAG (5-Feet High)

GOAL-POSTS & NET
(Posts 24 Feet Apart — Cross-Bar 8 Feet High)

CORNER FLAG (5-Feet High)

GOAL-LINE

GOAL-LINE

CORNER AREA (1-Yard Radius)

GOAL-AREA (6 x 20 Yards)

6-YARD LINE

CORNER AREA (1-Yard Radius)

PENALTY-AREA (18 x 44 Yards)

⊕ PENALTY-KICK-MARK (12 Yards From Goal-Line)

18-YARD LINE

PENALTY-ARC (10 Yards From Penalty-Kick-Mark)

"TOUCH"

TOUCH-LINE

TOUCH-LINE

"TOUCH"

HALFWAY-LINE

HALFWAY-LINE

CENTER-MARK

HALFWAY FLAG (Optional)

HALFWAY FLAG (Optional)

CENTER-CIRCLE (10 Yards From Center-Mark)

"TOUCH"

TOUCH-LINE

TOUCH-LINE

"TOUCH"

PENALTY-ARC (10 Yards From Penalty-Kick-Mark)

18-YARD LINE

PENALTY-AREA (18 x 44 Yards)

⊕ PENALTY-KICK-MARK (12 Yards From Goal-Line)

CORNER AREA (1-Yard Radius)

CORNER AREA (1-Yard Radius)

6-YARD LINE

GOAL-AREA (6 x 20 Yards)

GOAL-LINE

GOAL-LINE

GOAL-POSTS & NET
(Posts 24 Feet Apart — Cross-Bar 8 Feet High)

CORNER FLAG (5-Feet High)

CORNER FLAG (5-Feet High)

The Playing Field

Unlike most sports, the size and even the shape of a soccer field can vary. Its length can range from 100 to 130 yards, and its width can vary from 50 to 100 yards. Can a soccer field ever be a 100-yard by 100-yard square? No. It must always be longer than it is wide. In other words, it must always be a rectangle.

For FIFA-sanctioned international matches, the field must be between 110 to 120 yards long and 70 to 80 yards wide.

1. **THE MARKINGS:** All the lines on the field must be 5 inches or less in width. To prevent undo influence on the path of the ball, lines should not be rutted; they should be level with the field of play.

2. **THE TOUCH-LINES:** The lines marking the long sides of the field are called "touch-lines." Balls that have passed over these touch-lines may be "touched" or picked up in order to be thrown back into play. For this reason, the area outside the touch-lines is called "touch," and an out-of-bounds ball may be referred to as being "in-touch."

3. **THE GOAL-LINES:** The shorter lines marking the ends of the field are called "goal-lines." The two goals are erected directly atop these goal-lines.

4. **AREA BOUNDARIES:** The lines on the field are considered to be parts of the areas they enclose. For instance, the exact outer limit of the field is at the *outside edges* of the touch-lines and goal-lines, not at the centers of these lines, nor at their inner edges. In a similar way, the boundaries of the various circles, quarter circles and rectangles on the field are located at the *outer* edges of the lines marking them.

5. **THE FLAGS:** The four outer corners of the field are marked by corner-flags. These flags are used as visual indicators to help show when and how a ball has passed out-of-bounds. Optional flags may also be placed at mid-field. If these are used, they must stand at least 1 yard off the edge of the field. For safety's sake, all flagpoles must have blunt ends, and they must be at least 5 feet tall.

6. **THE CORNER-AREAS:** In each corner of the field, there is a small corner-area marked by a quarter-circle with a radius of 1 yard. The only purpose of the corner-areas is to show where the ball is to be placed for corner-kicks.

7. **THE HALFWAY MARKINGS:** The halfway markings are used mainly for kick-offs. The field is divided in half by a "halfway-line" running across its middle. During kick-offs, the two teams are required to stay on their own sides of the halfway-line. The middle of the halfway-line is marked by the center-mark. The ball is placed on the center-mark for kick-offs. The center-mark is surrounded by a center-circle of 10 yards radius. When a team is kicking off, opponents must stay outside of the center-circle. There is one other purpose for the halfway-line. In determining offside violations, a player cannot be called offside if he is on his own team's side of the halfway-line, *i.e.*, if he is in his own half of the field. See "The Offside-Rule," page 55.

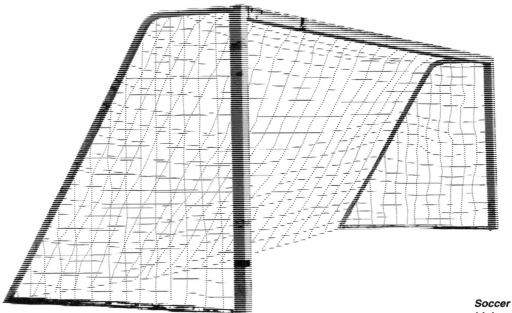

Soccer goals measure eight feet high and twenty-four feet wide.

8. **THE GOALS:** At each end of the field, there stands an upright, rectangular goal that measures 8 feet high by 24 feet wide (inside measurements). Each goal is outlined by two white goal-posts and a white horizontal cross-bar. These members must all be of equal thickness, and their thickness must be the same as the width of the goal-lines (maximum 5 inches). The cross-section of the goal-posts and cross-bar may be square, rectangular, round, oval or half-round. Usually, a net is suspended across the back of the goal to catch balls and help determine if a goal has been scored. If used, nets should be pulled back and supported so they don't restrict the players' movements.

9. **THE GOAL-AREAS:** Directly in front of each goal is a small marked rectangle called a goal-area. Each goal-area measures 6 by 20 yards. In addition to showing where the ball may be placed for goal-kicks, the goal-areas are sanctuaries for the goal-keepers, who are semi-protected

from charging within them. The lines marking the sides of the goal-areas closest to midfield are 6 yards from the goal-lines, and are called the six-yard-lines. See "The Goal-Keepers," page 16.

10. **THE PENALTY-AREAS:** Surrounding each goal-area is a larger rectangle called the penalty-area or "penalty-box." Each penalty-area measures 18 by 44 yards, and includes the goal-area within it. When a rule refers to an event occurring "within a penalty-area," it usually also means within the included goal-area. A goal-keeper may handle the ball when it is inside his own penalty-area (or the included goal-area). The lines marking the sides of the penalty-areas closest to midfield are 18 yards from the goal-lines, and are called the eighteen-yard-lines.

11. **THE PENALTY-KICK-MARKS:** If a team commits one of the 9 major-fouls within its own penalty-area, the opposing team is awarded a penalty-kick taken from the penalty-kick-mark in that penalty-area. The penalty-kick-marks are located 12 yards out from each goal, and they are centered on the goal-posts. During a penalty-kick, the ball is placed on the penalty-kick-mark, and a free shot on goal is taken, with only the opposing goal-keeper allowed to defend.

12. **THE PENALTY-ARCS:** Extending from each penalty-area is a semi-circular line called the penalty-arc. This arc marks a 10-yard distance from the penalty-kick-mark. During a penalty-kick, all players except the kicker and the defending goal-keeper must stay outside the penalty-arc, as well as outside the penalty-area and the included goal-area. The semi-circular areas marked by the penalty-arcs are not part of the penalty-areas. Penalty-kicks are not awarded for fouls committed within these arcs, nor may goal-keepers use their hands within them.

The Player Positions

A regulation FIFA team must have no more than 11 players. Usually, 7 is the minimum number of players allowed, although youth leagues sometimes specify smaller teams. Each team must designate one player who is called the goal-keeper, "goalie," or "keeper."

The Goal-Keepers

Although they are free to play anywhere on the field, the goal-keepers' main job is to defend their goals.

The goal-keepers are the only players allowed to use their hands and arms to touch the ball, and no player may kick at the ball while it is being held by a goal-keeper.

The goal-keepers' protection from physical contact depends on what part of the field they are playing in. This is a "gray area" of the *Laws of the Game.* Actual practice is different from what may be inferred from the written rules. See following section, "What Really Happens."

Within the penalty-area, the goal-keeper may play the ball with the hands and arms.

1. **ON THE OPEN FIELD:** When playing outside their own penalty-areas (and the included goal-areas), goal-keepers have no special privileges. They may not touch the ball with their hands and arms, and the rules apply to them just as to the other players.

2. **IN THEIR PENALTY-AREAS:** When the ball is within their own penalty-areas (and the included goal-areas), the goal-keepers are allowed to kick it or touch it with any part of their bodies, including their hands and arms. Here, the goal-keepers may catch the ball, hold it, or even run short distances with it. Once they have gained possession of the ball with their hands, goal-keepers must be allowed to release it back into play without interference.

3. **IN THEIR GOAL-AREAS:** Besides the ability to use their hands and arms, the official rules give goal-keepers special protection inside their own goal-areas. Here, for all practical purposes, they may not be fair-charged. Only minor, incidental body contact is allowed during a legitimate play for a loose ball. The official FIFA rules actually state that goal-keepers *may* be fair-charged when they have possession of the ball in their goal-areas, but this is not permitted in actual practice. Once the

goal-keeper has possession of the ball, he must be allowed to release it back into play without interference.

WHAT REALLY HAPPENS: In actual practice, the goal-keeper's protection from physical contact within the goal-area extends to the entire penalty-area as well. There is little, if any, difference in the way the rules are applied to the two areas. The exact degree to which goal-keepers are protected from physical contact within these areas varies slightly from one referee to another. Generally, however, the goal-keeper may not be interfered with while in the act of grabbing the ball, and he may not be interfered with while he is attempting to release the ball back into play. In both areas, only minor, incidental body contact is allowed during a legitimate play for a loose ball, *i.e.*, before the goal-keeper has grabbed it.

SPECIAL NOTE FOR YOUTH LEAGUES: Commonly, youth leagues specify that goal-keepers are protected from all fair-charging while within their own penalty-areas and the included goal-areas.

Goal-Keeper Limitations

Goal-keepers are subject to several limitations that apply only to them:

1. **FOUR-STEP-RULE:** Once they gain possession of the ball, goal-keepers may travel only four steps before they must release it back into play. Basketball-style hand dribbling and juggling the ball in the air are allowed, but may not be used to extend this distance. Traditionally, referees are lenient in allowing extra steps for the goal-keeper to regain his balance after a save.

2. **TIME-WASTING:** Goal-keepers must release the ball back into play promptly. Lying on the ball, or holding it for an unreasonable period will draw a penalty.

3. **DOUBLE-POSSESSION:** Once a goal-keeper has gained possession of the ball with his hands, he must release it back into play, and he may not possess it again with his hands until it is touched by an opponent anywhere on the field, or by a teammate outside the penalty-area.

Double-possession does not apply to playing the ball with the feet. The goal-keeper may dribble or kick the ball just as any other player, whether or not he has possessed it with his hands. Thus, he may catch the ball with his hands, place it on the ground, and then dribble it or kick it to a teammate. He may also gain control of a loose ball with his feet, dribble it for a while, and then pick it up. However, he may not possess the ball with his hands twice. Further, he may not handle the ball at all if it has been kicked to him by a teammate. See following section, "Kicking To The Keeper."

The goal-keeper's first possession is not counted until he has actually gained full control of the ball. If the ball gets loose while he is still trying to capture it, he may grab it again.

Having the ball trapped against the ground is counted as a "possession." The goal-keeper is also considered to have had a "possession" if he knocks the ball to the ground in a manner that allows him to play it

The goal-keeper may take a maximum of four steps before releasing the ball back into play.

with his feet. He is judged to have had possession if, in the opinion of the referee, he *could* have caught it. Dropping the ball and re-catching it, tapping along the ground with the hands, and rolling away and re-catching all count as double-possession.

4. **"KICKING-TO-THE-KEEPER":** This term is applied to a recent FIFA ruling that a goal-keeper may not touch the ball with his hands if it has been intentionally kicked to him by a teammate. (He may, however, play the ball with his feet.) The intention of this rule is to prevent undue time wasting by restricting the ability of the goal-keeper and his team-mates to "keep the ball away" from the other team. Technically, this rule only prohibits the goal-keeper from catching the ball when it has been *kicked* to him by a teammate. However, any trickery by the team-mate to circumvent the spirit of the rule, such as lifting the ball with the foot in order to head it to his goal-keeper, is penalized as ungentlemanly conduct by the teammate. It is legal for the goal-keeper to handle a ball that has been thrown to him during a throw-in, or to handle a ball that has been legitimately played to him by a teammate in some way other than by kicking. For example, a teammate may intercept a pass by an opponent by heading it to his own goal-keeper.

The Field Players

There are no official specifications for the field playing positions or how many players there may be in each position. "Goal-keeper" is the only position specified in the official FIFA rules. All of the other players are anonymous and completely interchangeable as far as the rules are concerned.

In contrast to the goal-keepers, the other players on the field may not touch the ball with the hands or arms. They may play the ball only by kicking it or striking it with other parts of the body, including the feet, legs, head, torso, and the *tops* of the shoulders. The sides of the shoulders, over the outer arm muscles, are considered to be parts of the arms.

Any player may use the hands to pick up an out-of-bounds ball, or to position the ball on the ground for a free-kick.

Traditionally, soccer field positions fall into three basic categories: full-back, halfback, and forward:

1. **THE FULLBACKS:** These are primarily defensive players stationed near the goal-keeper at the rear of a team's formation. As the team follows the ball up and down the field, the fullbacks usually remain at the rear. Sometimes, one of the fullbacks may be assigned to cover a specific attacker, or a fullback may be stationed very near the goal-keeper to act as a last line of defense. These specially-assigned fullbacks may have names such as "stopper-back" or "sweeper-back."

2. **THE HALFBACKS:** These are flexible players who are stationed in the middle of a team's formation. As the team follows the ball up and down the field, the halfbacks will remain in the center of the action. Their job is to gain possession of the ball and initiate attacks. They must be able to switch from defense to offense very quickly. Often, the center halfback is thought of as the leader of the team. Halfbacks are also called "midfielders."

3. **THE FORWARDS:** These are offensive players who are responsible for scoring goals. As the team moves up and down the field, the forwards

will play at the front of the formation, ready to spring to the attack at the first opportunity. The center forwards, also called "strikers," are thought of as the team's primary scorers. The side forwards are also called "wingers." They threaten to shoot from the sides, and attempt to make assist passes to the strikers.

Coaches, Trainers & Others

No one is allowed on the field without permission from the referee. Even for the treatment of injuries, the referee must give permission for trainers to enter the field. Special areas may be designated off the ends of the field for photographers and other observers. Coaching from the sidelines is permitted if conducted in a "responsible manner."

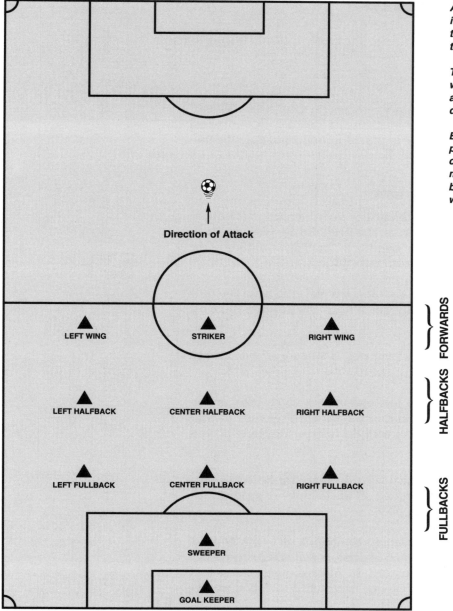

A typical soccer formation might include a goal-keeper, a sweeper, three fullbacks, three halfbacks and three forwards.

The opposing team (not shown) would have a similar formation arranged to attack in the opposite direction.

Except for the goal-keeper, all field players are anonymous and completely interchangeable. They may switch positions and responsibilities at any time, even "on the fly" while the game is in progress.

Infractions and Punishment

Soccer infractions are divided into three general categories: "Fouls," "Misconduct" and "Offside." These infractions are detailed in individual sections. A summary is presented here as an aid in understanding the mechanics of the game:

Infractions

1. **FOULS:** Fouls may be generally defined as improper action intentionally inflicted upon another player, on the field, during play, *e.g.,* tripping or spitting. Additionally, the "hand-ball," or illegal handling of the ball, is considered a foul. See "Fouls," page 45.

   Generally, only one foul is called at a time. If a player or team commits more than one foul simultaneously, the referee will penalize the most serious.

   If opponents foul each other simultaneously, the more serious may be penalized.

2. **MISCONDUCT VIOLATIONS:** Misconduct is a much broader category that includes violations against the spirit of the game, *e.g.,* time wasting, illegal procedure, arguing with the referee, too many players on the field.

   Misconduct also includes acts that would otherwise be considered "fouls," but that have been committed off the field; by or against non-players; or while the ball is not in play.

   Misconduct may be called for violations committed on or off the field, at any time, by players or substitutes. Spectators and other non-participants may not be called for misconduct. In youth soccer, coaches may be called for misconduct. More than one misconduct violation may be called at a time. See "Misconduct," page 53.

Pushing! Holding! Tripping! Striking! In soccer, most minor body contact during a legitimate play for the ball is considered "accidental," and thus part of normal play.

3. **OFFSIDE VIOLATIONS:** The complex Offside-Rule is based on the notion that it is unsporting for attacking players to hang around the mouth of the goal, waiting for a pass and an easy score. With many exceptions and qualifications, attacking players are therefore generally prohibited from positioning themselves ahead of the ball. See "The Offside-Rule," page 55.

Punishment

Punishment for soccer infractions comes in two general forms: free-kicks and referee sanctions:

1. **FREE-KICKS:** For a free-kick, the ball is placed stationary on the ground and a member of the offended team is allowed to kick it without interference from opponents. Free-kicks may be either "direct" or "indirect," the difference being whether or not a goal may be scored directly as a result of the initial kick. See "Free-Kicks," page 48.

   DIRECT-FREE-KICKS: A direct-free-kick may score if the ball passes directly through the opponents' goal, without being touched by any other player. Similar to this category is the "penalty-kick," a special kick that is not only "direct," but also has severe restrictions placed on the defense. A penalty-kick often results in a direct score by the kicking team.

   INDIRECT-FREE-KICKS: An indirect-free-kick may not score unless the ball is touched by a second player from either team after the initial kick.

2. **REFEREE SANCTIONS:** In addition to free-kicks, the referee may issue "cautions," or "ejections" to offending players and substitutes.

Informal verbal reprimands may also be made by the referee for minor infractions. This type of warning carries no penalty, and may be issued "on the fly" without interruption of the game.

CAUTIONS (YELLOW-CARD): A formal "caution" must be issued while play is stopped. The referee will raise a yellow-card over his head to indicate that the caution has been issued, and will record the player's number.

Note: A player may continue to play after receiving a single caution, but not with two cautions. If he receives a second caution, he is immediately ejected from the game. The referee will briefly show the yellow-card, and then immediately eject the player by raising the red-card, as explained below.

EJECTIONS (RED-CARD): An "ejection" or "send-off" may also only be issued while play is stopped. The referee will raise a red-card over his head to indicate that the ejection has occurred. An ejected player must leave the field immediately, and may not be replaced.

Fitting Punishment To The Crime

The following general guidelines are used to determine which penalties will be applied to the various types of infractions.

1. **MAJOR-FOULS:** A **direct-free-kick** or **penalty-kick** is awarded to the fouled team. The penalty-kick is awarded in case a team commits a major-foul within its own penalty-area.

2. **MINOR-FOULS:** An **indirect-free-kick** is awarded to the fouled team.

3. **OFFSIDE VIOLATIONS:** An **indirect-free-kick** is awarded to the opposing team.

4. **MAJOR-MISCONDUCT VIOLATIONS:** An **ejection** (red-card) is issued to the offending player.

5. **MINOR-MISCONDUCT VIOLATIONS:** A **caution** (yellow-card) is issued to the offending player. If he commits a second cautionable offense, the yellow-card is shown, immediately followed by an **ejection** (red-card).

It is important to note that there is considerable overlap between the penalties imposed for fouls and misconduct. For example, the referee may decide that a particularly grievous foul is severe enough to merit an immediate misconduct ejection, as well as a free-kick. Also, if the referee whistles the ball dead in order to issue punishment for misconduct, play is resumed with an indirect-free-kick awarded to the offended team, just as though a minor-foul had been committed. See individual sections on "Fouls," page 45; "The Offside-Rule," page 55; and "Misconduct," page 53.

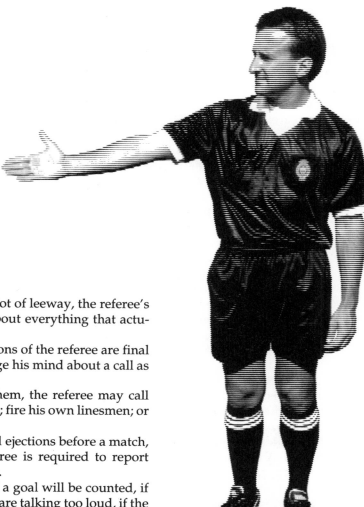

The Referee

Because the rules intentionally allow him at lot of leeway, the referee's *interpretations* of those rules will determine just about everything that actually occurs during a match.

From the moment he takes the field, the decisions of the referee are final and incontestable. However, the referee may change his mind about a call as long as play has not resumed.

For infractions of the rules as he interprets them, the referee may call fouls; eject players; remove coaches and substitutes; fire his own linesmen; or even terminate the game.

The referee has authority to issue penalties and ejections before a match, during it, and during any rest periods. The referee is required to report violations to the league or other proper authorities.

The referee decides if the field is fit for play, if a goal will be counted, if the players' uniforms are acceptable, if the coaches are talking too loud, if the players are behaving in a sportsmanlike manner, etc., etc.

Last but not least, the referee is time keeper for the game.

The referee is responsible for preserving order, the spirit of the game, and the safety of the players.

More than in any other major team sport, the soccer referee is empowered to control the ebb and flow of action on the field.

General Philosophy

The spirit of the rules is that soccer games should proceed with as little interruption as possible. Generally, the referee should stop play only when it is necessary to preserve order, the spirit of the game, or the safety of the players.

The official FIFA rules say it best: "Constant whistling for trifling and doubtful breaches produces bad feeling and loss of temper on the part of the players and spoils the pleasure of spectators."

Referee Discretion

The rules are specific as to what type of punishment is to be given for each type of violation. However, the final decision as to whether the punishment, if any, is to be given is up to the discretion of the referee. The crucial factors are: the severity of the violation, the degree of premeditation, and the balance of playing advantage between the fouling team and the offended team. Taking all of these factors into mind, the referee may ignore the foul, award the specified form of free-kick; issue a caution, or ejection; or some combination.

Judging Intention

An important consideration in the referee's decision on whether or not to penalize a foul is the degree of premeditation involved.

In increasing order, the three degrees of premeditation in committing a soccer foul are: Accidental, Intentional, and Deliberate.

1. **ACCIDENTAL FOULS:** An accidental foul is committed in complete innocence while trying to make a legal play; accidental fouls are not generally penalized. For example, while a player is attempting to kick the ball, a defender may suddenly stick his leg out so that the leg gets kicked, rather than the ball. There was no time for the first player to see the leg and avoid kicking it, and no penalty is called.

2. **INTENTIONAL FOULS:** An intentional foul is committed with the knowledge that it is going to happen, but with the main intent being to play the ball. An intentional foul may be disguised as an attempt to play the ball, but with the knowledge that a foul may also occur. Taking the first example, assume that the kicking player sees the defender's leg and knows that it will be struck, but kicks at the ball anyway, leg or no leg. A penalty is called.

3. **DELIBERATE FOULS:** The primary intent of a deliberate foul is to commit the foul, not to play the ball. Again taking the first example, assume that the kicker sees the defender and realizes he has no chance to play the ball, so he decides to remove the defender altogether by tripping him from behind. A penalty is called in addition to a probable caution or ejection.

Although fouls must generally be intentional for the call to be made, actual contact is not absolutely necessary. With the exception of the hand-ball, the mere *attempt* to commit the foul may be sufficient grounds to issue a penalty.

The Advantage-Clause

A major element of the referee's decision-making authority is something called the "Advantage-Clause."

This states that even when an obvious, indisputable foul has been committed, the referee may choose to ignore the foul and let play continue without calling a penalty.

Why would the referee do this?

It is because the fouled team may still have the better playing position (or "advantage") at that moment, despite the foul. To stop play for a penalty would nullify the fouled team's advantage and do it even more harm.

The idea of the "Advantage-Clause" is to give the fouled team the best chance by letting play continue if it has the playing "advantage."

Applying the Advantage-Clause is a source of controversy during soccer games, because it is often a matter of opinion as to whether or not the fouled team actually has the advantage.

When the referee decides not to penalize a foul, he will extend both hands and call, "Advantage! Play On!," or simply "Play On!," letting every-one know that he has seen the foul and why he is ignoring it. This is

"Play On!" The referee extends both hands to signal that he has chosen to ignore a foul and let play continue without interruption.

important to game control because fouled players might otherwise decide to take matters into their own hands and retaliate.

Even when the referee has invoked the Advantage-Clause, he may still wish to caution or eject the offending player. In that case, he will wait for a natural pause in play before imposing the penalty.

However, the referee may not award a free-kick at a later time. If he wishes to award a free-kick, he must stop play immediately.

One effect of the Advantage-Clause is that play should not stop just because an obvious foul is committed. The referee may not see it, or he may choose to invoke the Advantage-Clause. Players should continue to play until they hear the whistle.

The Linesmen

The referee is usually assisted by two linesmen who run up and down the touch-lines signalling with small hand flags. Depending on the level of play, the linesmen may be volunteers from the two sides, or they may be trained referees themselves who work as a unit with the center referee:

1. **CLUB-LINESMEN:** Volunteer linesmen are called club-linesmen, and their duties are usually limited to signalling when the ball has passed out-of-bounds and which team last touched it.

2. **NEUTRAL-LINESMEN:** Trained linesmen are called neutral-linesmen, and their duties may include signalling offside violations, substitutions, fouls, or even when a goal has been scored. Linesmen do not actually make calls; they only use their flags to signal their opinions to the referee. In all cases, the level of responsibility assumed by the linesmen is determined by the referee, and the referee will decide whether or not to make the call.

Officiating Systems

Officiating systems for soccer matches usually involve a combination of referees on the field and linesmen on the touch-lines. In all systems, it is essential that the officials work together as a team to ensure that all parts of the field are covered.

1. **THE DIAGONAL SYSTEM:** Many adult soccer matches are officiated by a single referee and two neutral-linesmen. The referee runs on a diagonal path from corner to corner, across the center of the

The neutral-linesman's flag signal that a foul has been observed on the field.

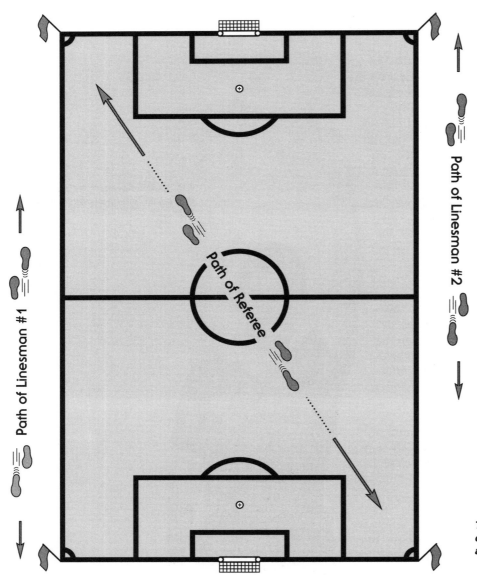

The Diagonal System of game officiating uses two neutral-linesmen and a referee to cover the field.

field, and a neutral-linesman is stationed on each touch-line. Each neutral-linesman is responsible for the triangular section of the field on his side of the referee's diagonal running path. The linesmen assist in signalling calls.

2. **THE ONE REFEREE SYSTEM:** When no neutral-linesmen are available, two club-linesmen may be used in conjunction with a single referee who runs a rough "X-shaped" pattern in the center of the field. The club-linesmen are used primarily to indicate out-of-bounds, with the referee making all calls independently. This is the most common system for youth games.

3. **MULTI-REFEREE SYSTEMS:** These systems employ two or even three referees on the field and no linesmen. The referees share varying territories and degrees of authority.

Equipment

One of the reasons soccer is so popular around the world is that so little equipment is required to play the game. A ball, a whistle, basic uniforms, and a grassy field with two simple rectangular goals are all that are really necessary to have a soccer match.

The Ball

Soccer balls are spherical, with a circumference of 27 to 28 inches. They should weigh 14 to 16 ounces, and they should be inflated at 8.5 to 15.6 pounds per square inch of air pressure. Firm, but not hard.

The ball is usually made of leather or a similar material, and is traditionally covered with a pattern of alternating white hexagons and black pentagons.

The referee must approve of the ball prior to the game, and of any changes of the ball during a game.

Youth leagues may use smaller balls, depending on the age of the players. These balls may weigh as little as 10 ounces, and may have a circumference of as little as 23 inches.

The Uniform

Required uniform items include a shirt, shorts, shoes, stockings, and shin guards. The shin guards must be completely covered by the stockings.

Traditionally, players' shirts are numbered and team members wear matching colors. Numbers may not be changed during a match except when changing shirts with the goal-keeper.

The two goal-keepers must wear colors that distinguish them not only from both teams, but also from each other, and from the officials as well.

Referees and linesmen wear colors that distinguish them from both teams, traditionally black with white trim.

Cleats are allowed on shoes as long as they are not dangerous in the opinion of the referee. Players may not wear or carry any-

thing dangerous to other players. No foreign objects may be carried or used during the match. Jewelry, casts, eye glasses, etc., are subject to the approval of the referee.

Uniform Problems

Before the game, the referee will check for improper items. A player will not be permitted to play with improper wear.

Once the game has begun, a player with improper wear may be required to leave the game. This may only take place during a natural stoppage of play. The referee will not normally stop play to correct a uniform problem.

A player removed because of a uniform problem may return to the match only during a natural stoppage of play, and only after the referee has checked his uniform and has given permission. Or, the player's team may send in a substitute for him, subject to the normal limitations on substitution. See "Substitutions," page 63.

Referee Items

The referee carries several items used in officiating the game:

1. A coin used for the opening coin-toss.

2. A whistle used to stop play when necessary.

3. A watch carried to keep official time for the game.

4. A pencil and a notebook or game card to record goals, penalties, and other information for the sanctioning league.

5. Two small cards measuring about 3 by 5 inches. One card is yellow, and the other is red. These cards are displayed to indicate when the referee has called a formal caution (yellow-card) or an ejection (red-card).

The Linesmen's Flags

The two linesmen each carry a small, brightly-colored flag used for signalling. Traditionally, these flags measure about 1 foot square, and are mounted on short sticks about 18 inches long.

Beginning The Game

The referee will make sure that all conditions are proper for the match. He will meet with his linesmen and inspect the field, the markings, the goals, nets, posts, and the game ball.

The field should be firm enough so that the ball will bounce when dropped from chest height, and visibility should allow one side of the field to be seen from the other.

The referee will call the teams to the center of the field for a brief conference, uniform inspection, identification of team captains, and the coin-toss.

The Coin-Toss

To determine which team will kick off, the referee or the captain of the home team will toss a coin. Traditionally, the captain of the visiting team makes the call.

The team that wins the coin-toss may chose to kick off, or it may chose which end of the field to defend. Usually, it will chose to attack immediately by taking the kick-off, and the other team is then allowed to decide which end of the field it will defend.

Because of lighting or weather conditions, the team that wins the coin-toss may elect to chose which end of the

Traditionally, the visiting captain makes the call.

field it will defend. If that happens, the other team gets to kick off. Immediately after the toss, the teams take up their positions, and the referee will whistle for the kick-off to take place.

The Kick-Off (or "Place-Kick")

Kick-offs are used to begin the game; to restart play after each goal is scored; to restart play after half-time; and to begin overtime periods.

(Note: Most precisely, the term "kick-off" is refers to the taking of the initial kick to begin or restart play. The kick itself is called a "place-kick." Here, all kicks — or the taking of all kicks — from the center-mark to begin or restart play will simply be called "kick-offs.")

1. The ball is placed stationary on the center-mark.

2. Both teams must remain on their own sides of the center-line until the ball is kicked.

3. Opponents of the kicker must remain at least 10 yards from the ball until it is kicked. This distance is marked by the center-circle. The kicker's teammates may position themselves any distance from the ball (even inside the center-circle), as long as they are on their own half of the field.

4. The kicker must wait for a signal from the referee.

5. The ball must travel forward across the center-line into the defenders' half of the field.

6. A kick-off is "indirect," since no goal can be scored until a second player from either team touches the ball.

7. The ball is in play at the moment it has traveled forward one full revolution, about 28 inches.

8. A re-kick is taken if the ball fails to enter play legally.

9. Once the ball is in play, the kicker may not play it again until it is touched by another player. This is double-play, punished by the awarding of an indirect-free-kick to the opposing team.

10. Repeated procedural violations may be treated as misconduct if intentional.

Keeping Time

A regulation game is broken into two, 45-minute halves, with a 5-minute half-time break. The referee is required to allow a break between periods if requested by any player. Youth games are typically shorter, and they may be divided into as many as four periods. Official game time is kept according to the following rules:

1. The referee is the sole official time keeper for the match, and he carries at least one watch for that purpose. Any "game clocks" on display for the players and spectators show only an *unofficial estimate* of the time remaining. The official "clock" (actually a watch) may be stopped and started only by the referee, and only the referee knows the exact moment when time runs out.

The referee is sole timekeeper for the match.

2. There are no team "time outs" allowed.

3. At the opening kick-off, the referee's watch is started at the moment the ball is properly put into play. Once started, time runs more or less continuously to the end of the period.

4. Time is not stopped for short interruptions. This includes out-of-bounds balls, penalties, minor injuries, etc.

5. The referee may choose to "stop the clock" for significant interruptions. These might include: substitutions, major injuries, lost or defective balls, or time-wasting by the leading team. The amount of time added to the game is up to the discretion of the referee.

6. The game or period ends at the exact moment when time runs out. If a shot is in mid-air when time runs out, no goal is possible.

7. A period or game may end while the ball is out of play, *e.g.*, while the players are lining up for a corner-kick.

8. However, time may not run out with a penalty-kick pending. If a foul justifying a penalty-kick is committed just as time runs out, the referee will extend time enough to allow the kick to be taken. See "Penalty-Kicks," page 50.

Out-Of-Bounds

The ball becomes "dead" automatically when it passes out-of-bounds. It is immediately put back into play with practically no interruption in the flow of the game.

Although no whistle is required for an out-of-bounds dead-ball, the referee may choose to "whistle the ball dead" in questionable cases.

DEFINITION: The ball can go out-of-bounds either by passing over a touch-line; or by passing over a goal-line without entering one of the goals. (This includes flying off the field over the top on a goal.)

Also treated as "out-of-bounds" are balls that do enter the goals, but at times when scoring is not technically possible, *e.g.*, during a kick-off.

The ball remains in play as long as *any part* of it remains over the field. Because the touch-lines and goal-lines themselves are considered to be part of the field, *all* of the ball must pass completely beyond the *outside* edges of these lines for it to be out-of-bounds.

The ball is still in play as long as even the tiniest part of it remains above any part of the line.

Because the goal-posts, cross-bars, and corner-flags are on the field, a ball striking one of them and bouncing back onto the field is still in play.

A ball that strikes a referee or linesman on the field is still in play, unless it bounces out-of-bounds.

Note: A ball that completely leaves the field and follows a curving path that brings it back onto the field is still out-of-bounds. This is true whether the ball is rolling or flying through the air.

The throw-in must be two-handed, and the throw must be from directly over and behind the head.

WHO GETS THE BALL?: The ball is immediately put back into play by the *opponents* of the team that last touched it before it went out-of-bounds.

This rule is followed even if the last contact with the ball was passive or accidental. For instance, if a player on Team A kicks the ball, and it hits a Team B player in the back and bounces out-of-bounds, Team A is allowed to put the ball into play. The deciding factor is that the ball last touched someone from Team B.

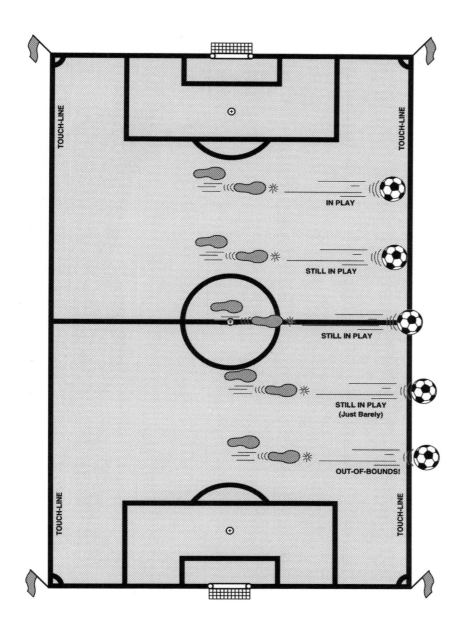

The ball is still in play as long as even the tiniest part of it remains over the line.

There are three methods of putting a ball back into play, depending on *where* it went out-of-bounds and *who* last touched it:

Out-Of-Bounds Over A Touch-Line
(Throw-In)

Regardless of which team last touches the ball, if it goes out-of-bounds over a touch-line, it is put back into play with a throw-in by the opposing team.

1. The referee or a linesman will signal for out-of-bounds balls by pointing in the attacking direction of the team that is to put the ball into play. Players are expected to put the ball into play without further guidance or delay.

2. The throw must be made from within about a yard of the point where the ball left the field. Some minor "fudging" up and down the touch-line is usually allowed (but no more than about a yard). Any member of the throwing team may take the throw.

3. Opponents and the thrower's teammates may station themselves where they wish; there is no specific distance requirement. Opponents may not dance about, gesticulate or otherwise distract the thrower.

4. The throw may be made immediately, without pause in play or permission from the referee. It is not necessary to wait for opponents to move back.

5. The throw must be a standing, two-handed throw, from straight over and behind the head, with both feet touching the ground, and equal force used with both hands. The feet may be spread apart sideways or front-to-back.

6. At least part of *both feet* must be in contact with the touch-line or the ground just outside the touch-line. (If only the heel of the foot is on the touch-line, it must maintain contact with the ground during the throw.)

7. The thrower must face the field and *throw* the ball in a forward direction, not just drop it.

8. Acrobatic or running starts are allowed as long as a legal position is attained at the instant of release.

9. The ball must enter the field while flying through the air. It may not be bounced in or rolled in.

10. The ball is in play at the instant the thrower releases it, and any part of it passes over the touch-line. There is no minimum distance requirement.

11. A throw-in is "indirect," since no goal can be scored until a second player from either team touches the ball.

12. Some referees may consider it a legal tactic to throw the ball so that it bounces non-violently off an opponent. If allowed, the ball may then be played again by the thrower.

13. The Offside-Rule does not apply during the initial throw, *i.e.*, it is not possible for the first player to touch the ball after the throw to be called offside. See "The Offside-Rule," page 55.

14. Once the ball is in play, the thrower may not play it again until it has been touched by another player. This is double-play, punished by giving an indirect-free-kick to the opposing team.

15. If the thrower makes an improper throw that enters play, then the opposing team is awarded the ball, and immediately puts it back into play with a throw-in from the same spot.

For an out-of-bounds ball over a touch-line, the linesman will use his flag to point in the attacking direction of the team that is to put the ball back into play.

16. However, if the ball fails to enter play legally, a re-throw is taken by the same team.

17. Repeated procedural violations may be treated as misconduct if intentional.

Out-Of-Bounds Over A Goal-Line
(Goal-Kick or Corner-Kick)

If the ball is driven out-of-bounds over a goal-line, there are two types of kicks that may be used to put it back into play: "goal-kicks" or "corner-kicks."

The type of kick awarded depends on which team last touched the ball.

GOAL-KICKS: When any player last touches the ball before it goes out-of-bounds over the **opposing team's goal-line** (*e.g.*, he misses a shot on goal), then the opposing team puts the ball back into play with a goal-kick from its goal-area.

1. The referee will point to the goal-area to indicate that a goal-kick is to be taken.

2. The ball is placed stationary on the ground anywhere in the goal-area, so that at least part of it is within the outer edge of the goal-area boundary. Any player on the kicking team may place the ball, and any player may kick it.

3. Opponents of the kicker are required to remain entirely outside of the penalty-area and the included goal-area until the ball has left the penalty-area. The kicker's teammates may station themselves any place on the field.

4. The kick may be made immediately, without pause in play or permission from the referee. It is not necessary to wait for opponents to move back.

The referee will point briefly to the proper area to indicate that a goal-kick or a corner-kick is to be taken.

5. If an opponent of the kicker enters the penalty-area before the ball leaves, the referee may either allow play to continue (see "The Advantage-Clause," page 24), or have the kick retaken and caution the encroacher.

6. The ball may be kicked in any direction into the field of play.

7. The ball is in play at the moment it leaves the penalty-area and enters the field of play. It may not be played until it leaves the penalty-area. If it fails to leave the penalty-area, a re-kick is taken.

8. A goal-kick is "indirect," since no goal can be scored until a second player from either team touches the ball.

9. The Offside-Rule does not apply during the initial kick, *i.e.*, it is not possible for the first player to touch the ball after the initial kick to be called offside. See "The Offside-Rule," page 55.

10. Once the ball is in play, the kicker may not touch it again until it has been touched by another player. This is double-play, punishable by the awarding of an indirect-free-kick to the opposing team. For double-play committed before the ball enters play, *i.e.*, before it has left the penalty-area, a re-kick is taken.

11. A re-kick is taken if the ball fails to enter play by leaving the penalty-area and entering the field of play. This includes cases when the ball goes into the kicker's own goal; or if it goes out of bounds over that portion of the goal-line that borders the penalty-area.

12. Repeated procedural violations may be treated as misconduct if intentional.

CORNER-KICKS: When any player last touches the ball before it goes out-of-bounds over **his own goal-line** (*e.g.*, he deflects an opponent's shot over the top of his own goal), then the opposing team puts the ball back into play with a corner-kick taken from the nearest corner-area.

1. The referee will point to the corner where the kick is to be taken.

2. The ball is placed stationary on the ground so that its entirety is within the outer edges of the corner-area. Any player on the kicking team may place the ball, and any player may kick it.

3. Opponents of the kicker are required to remain 10 yards from the ball until it is kicked. Teammates may station themselves any place on the field.

4. The kick may be made immediately, without pause in play or permission from the referee. It is not necessary to wait for opponents to move back.

5. The corner-flags may not be moved in order to make a corner-kick easier.

6. The ball is in play when it has traveled one full revolution.

7. A corner-kick is "direct" in the sense that the ball may score if it passes directly through the opponents' goal without being touched by a second player.

8. The Offside-Rule does not apply during the initial kick, *i.e.*, it is not possible for the first player to touch the ball after the initial kick to be called offside. See "The Offside-Rule," page 55.

9. Once the ball is in play, the kicker may not touch it again until it has been touched by another player. This is double-play, punished by giving an indirect-free-kick to the opposing team.

10. The referee will check the position of the ball and corner-flag prior to the kick to make sure that it is taken properly.

11. Repeated procedural violations may be treated as misconduct if intentional.

For the corner-kick, the ball must be placed so that its entirety is within the outer edge of the corner-area.

Out-Of-Bounds Over A Corner-Flag

If the ball goes out-of-bounds over the exact corner of the field, *e.g.*, after pushing down a corner-flag, a decision must be made whether to treat the ball as though it has gone out-of-bounds over a goal-line, or over a touch-line.

Generally, the ball is put back into play in a manner that will give the greatest advantage to the defending team, *i.e.*, the team in whose half of the field the out-of-bounds occurred.

If the defending team last touched the ball, the attacking team is allowed to put it back into play, but with a throw-in rather than a corner-kick, which would threaten the possibility of a direct score.

Conversely, if the attackers last touched the ball, the defense puts it back into play with a clearing goal-kick, rather than a throw-in, which would risk a counter-attack near its own goal.

Questionable Out-Of-Bounds

If the ball goes out-of-bounds after being simultaneously touched by both teams, or if it is not possible to determine who last touched it, the referee may make an arbitrary choice, usually in favor of the defending team, and award a throw-in or goal-kick. It is also possible that the referee may call for a drop-ball in some cases. For example, if a drop-ball goes untouched out-of-bounds or through a goal, play is restarted with another drop-ball.

Intentional Out-Of-Bounds

Intentionally kicking the ball out-of-bounds is allowed as a tactical maneuver. However, if this is done as a means of wasting time, the referee may add time to the game to replace the time wasted.

The Drop-Ball

The drop-ball is used to restart the game after it has been stopped by the referee for some reason not directly attributable to the play of either team.

The drop-ball is also used as an "all-purpose" method of restarting play after it has been stopped for any reason not specifically covered in the *Laws of the Game*.

An important difference between drop-balls and all other forms of putting the ball into play is that during a drop-ball, it is the *referee* who puts the ball into play, not a player. This difference has an influence on the rules as applied to drop-balls:

1. The referee will usually call, "Drop-Ball," and pause a short moment to give the teams a chance to prepare themselves.

2. However, the referee may drop the ball *at any time* without warning. There is no explicit requirement that a player from each team be at the drop point, although the referee will usually hold onto the ball until both teams are ready.

3. The drop-ball is taken at the location of the ball at the moment play was stopped, unless the ball was inside one of the goal-areas. In that case, the drop-ball is taken as close as possible to the location of the ball at the last point of play, but on the six-yard line.

4. There is no specific distance the players must stay away. They may be as close to the drop point as desired, as long as they do not obstruct one another.

5. The referee will hold the ball out at waist level, and drop it to the ground vertically.

6. The ball is in play at the moment it touches the ground. No player may touch the ball until it hits the ground.

7. Since the ball is instantly in regular play when it touches the ground, it may score if it is then kicked directly through either goal.

For the drop-ball, the referee will usually wait until the opposing teams have prepared themselves.

8. The Offside-Rule does not apply during the drop, *i.e.*, it is not possible for the first player to touch the ball to be called offside. The Offside-Rule begins to apply at the moment the ball is touched. Therefore, the *second* player to touch the ball may be called offside. See "The Offside-Rule," page 55.

9. The double-play restriction does not apply, because the ball is actually put into play by the referee. The first player to touch the ball may dribble it, or contact it as many times as desired.

10. A goal-keeper within his own penalty-area may grab a drop-ball after it has touched the ground.

11. A re-drop is taken if the ball is touched before it contacts the ground, or if the ball goes untouched out-of-bounds, or if it goes untouched through either goal (unlikely).

12. Repeated procedural violations may be treated as misconduct if intentional.

Dead-Balls & Restarts

Even though the clock is usually not stopped, play is temporarily suspended when the referee "whistles the ball dead."

The ball becomes dead at the instant the referee whistles, even if this occurs when the ball is in mid-air. If the ball goes out-of-bounds or goes through a goal after a whistle, there is no play. The ball was already "dead," even though its motion continued afterwards.

After whistling to stop play, the referee must give some sort of signal to restart the game. This can be a gesture, a word, or the blowing of the whistle.

Summarized below are some reasons why the ball may be whistled dead, and for each reason the method of restarting play is given:

1. **GOAL SCORED:** The opposing team kicks off.

2. **OUT-OF-BOUNDS:** The ball is put back into play by the opponents of the team that last touched it. See "Out-Of-Bounds," page 32.

3. **FOUL CALLED:** The offended team is awarded the appropriate form of free-kick.

4. **MISCONDUCT WHISTLE:** If the referee stops the game to issue a caution or ejection, the opposing team is awarded either an indirect-free-kick, or a direct-free-kick or penalty-kick if a major-foul was involved. See "Misconduct," page 53.

5. **MISCONDUCT WHISTLE DURING DEAD-BALL:** If the referee whistles a caution or ejection during a dead-ball, the ball is put into play in a manner appropriate to the original dead-ball.

6. **NON-PLAYER MISCONDUCT:** If misconduct is committed by a non-player, such as a substitute on the bench, a drop-ball is taken from the location of the ball at the last point of play.

7. **IMPROPER THROW-IN:** The opposing team puts the ball back into play with a throw-in from the same spot. If the ball never entered play (*e.g.*, it slips backwards out of the thrower's hands), a re-throw is taken by the same team.

8. **PROCEDURAL FAILURE:** A re-take by the same team is given for failure to put the ball into play during a kick-off, goal-kick, corner-kick, throw-in, or any free-kick. A re-take may also be given in the event a player from the opposing team encroaches at those times.

9. **MAJOR INJURY BUT NO FOUL COMMITTED:** A drop-ball is taken from the location of the ball at the time of the whistle.

10. **EQUIPMENT PROBLEM:** Examples: Broken goal-post, corner-flag down, failed lighting. A drop-ball is taken from the location of the ball at the time of the whistle.

11. **ILLEGAL SUBSTITUTE ENTERS FIELD:** A drop-ball is taken from the location of the ball at the time of the whistle.

12. **OUTSIDE AGENT:** If a dog, spectator, or some other outside agent interrupts play or causes an out-of-bounds, a drop-ball is taken from the location of the ball at the time of the whistle.

13. **OFF-FIELD WHISTLE:** If players hear a whistle off the field and pause, the referee may call out "Keep Playing!" and play continues.

14. **REFEREE WHISTLE IN ERROR:** If the referee whistles unintentionally, or whistles improperly when not called for, and play stops, a drop-ball is taken from the location of the ball at the time of the whistle.

15. **END OF PERIOD:** The referee blows his whistle. The teams reverse ends of the field. A kick-off is taken by the opponents of the team that kicked off to begin the previous period. (Some referees may blow the whistle twice to signal the end of the first period.)

16. **END OF GAME:** The referee blows his whistle. No re-start. (Some referees may blow the whistle three times and point to the center-mark at the end of the game.)

Scoring Goals

Each team defends the goal at its end of the field while attempting to drive the ball through the other team's goal.

In order to score, the *entire* ball must pass through the goal and beyond the outer edge of the goal-line. The ball is still in play as long as any part of it remains over any part of the line.

A ball that flies over the cross-bar rather than into the goal is considered to have gone out-of bounds (no score). Following are some special scoring situations that may occur during a game:

1. **PLAYER SCORING AGAINST HIS OWN TEAM:** It is entirely possible for a player to score accidentally against his own team, but only during regular play. See following sections.

2. **DURING A KICK-OFF:** A kick-off is "indirect" since no goal can be scored until a second player from either team touches the ball.

   Should the ball pass directly through the opposing team's goal, it is considered to have gone out-of-bounds. The opposing team puts it into play with a goal-kick.

   A team may not score against itself during the initial kick because the ball is not in play unless it travels forward into the opponents' half of the field.

3. **GOAL-KEEPER HOLDING BALL:** A goal may be scored if the goal-keeper falls backwards into his own goal while he has the ball in his hands. A goal is counted as long as *the ball itself* passes completely into the goal, *i.e.*, completely over the goal-line, between the goal-posts, and under the cross-bar.

4. **GOAL-KEEPER RELEASE:** After making a "save" by stopping a shot by the opposing team, the goal-keeper releases the ball back into play with a clearing throw or kick. At this time, a goal may in theory be scored, if the ball passes directly through the opposing team's goal. Also, because the release is considered to be a form of "regular play," the goal-keeper may also score against himself at this time if he accidentally throws or swings the ball backwards into his own goal.

5. DURING DIRECT-FREE-KICKS: A direct-free-kick may score if the ball passes directly through the opponents' goal, without being touched by any other player.

Should the ball pass directly through the kicker's own goal, it is considered to have gone out-of-bounds, and the opposing team puts it into play with a corner-kick.

If the ball is touched by a second player from either team after the initial kick, it is considered to be in regular play, and may score if it then goes through *either* goal.

6. DURING INDIRECT-FREE-KICKS: An indirect-free-kick may not score unless the ball is touched by a second player from either team after the initial kick.

Should the ball pass untouched through either goal, it is considered to have gone out-of-bounds. The opposing team puts it into play with a goal-kick if the ball goes through its own goal, or with a corner-kick if the ball goes through the kicking team's goal.

If the ball is touched by a second player from either team after the initial kick, it is considered to be in regular play, and may score if it then goes through *either* goal.

7. DURING CORNER-KICKS: A corner-kick is "direct" in the sense that the ball may score if it goes directly through the opponents' goal without being touched by a second player.

8. DURING GOAL-KICKS: A goal-kick is "indirect" since no goal can be scored until a second player from either team touches the ball.

Should the ball pass directly through the opposing team's goal, it is considered to have gone out-of-bounds. The opposing team puts it into play with a goal-kick.

A team may not score against itself during the initial kick because the ball is not in play until it has left the penalty-area and entered the field of play. If the ball should go directly into the kicker's own goal without ever entering play, a re-kick is taken.

If the ball enters play, and is touched by a second player from either team, it is considered to be in regular play, and may score if it then goes through *either* goal.

9. DURING THROW-INS: A throw-in is "indirect," since the ball may not score unless touched by a second player from either team after the throw. Should the ball pass directly through either goal, it is considered

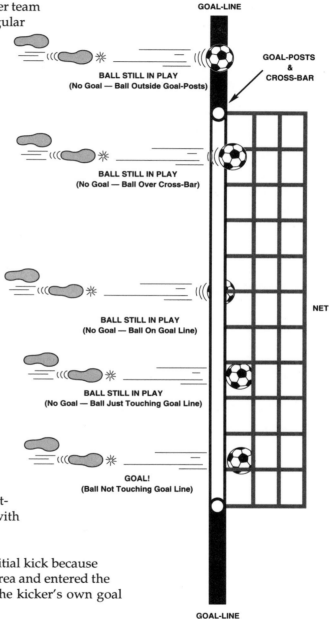

GOAL-LINE

GOAL-POSTS & CROSS-BAR

BALL STILL IN PLAY
(No Goal — Ball Outside Goal-Posts)

BALL STILL IN PLAY
(No Goal — Ball Over Cross-Bar)

NET

BALL STILL IN PLAY
(No Goal — Ball On Goal Line)

BALL STILL IN PLAY
(No Goal — Ball Just Touching Goal Line)

GOAL!
(Ball Not Touching Goal Line)

GOAL-LINE

To score, the entire ball must pass beyond the outer edge of the goal-line, between the goal-posts, and under the cross-bar.

to have gone out-of-bounds. The opposing team puts it into play with a goal-kick if the ball goes through its own goal, or with a corner-kick if the ball goes through the throwing team's goal.

If the ball is touched by a second player from either team after the initial throw, it is considered to be in regular play, and may score if it then goes through *either* goal.

10. **DURING DROP-BALLS:** The ball is considered to be instantly in regular play at the moment it contacts the ground. It may score if it is then kicked through *either* goal. However, if the ball should go untouched out-of-bounds, or if it should go untouched through either goal (unlikely), the ball is considered to have gone out-of-bounds. Play is restarted with another drop-ball.

11. **CONCURRENTLY WITH A FOUL:** If a *defender* commits a foul as a shot on goal is taken, but the ball enters the goal anyway, the referee will usually invoke the Advantage-Clause, ignore the infraction, and allow the goal to stand.

   If an infraction is committed by the *attacking* team, however, the referee will disallow the goal, and call a penalty.

12. **INTERFERENCE BY AN OUTSIDE AGENT:** A goal cannot be scored if the ball was last touched by an outside agent, *e.g.*, a spectator, dog, or bird. A drop-ball is taken, unless the interference occurs while the ball is in flight during a penalty-kick. In that case, a re-kick is taken.

   Note: The goals, the corner-flags and the referee are not considered to be outside agents, but part of the field. A ball may score if it enters a goal after bouncing off one of them.

13. **UNAUTHORIZED PLAYERS:** If an extra player or unauthorized substitute is discovered after a goal has been scored and the ensuing kick-off has already taken place, the goal must be allowed to stand.

Fouls

"Dangerous-play," a minor-foul.

As explained in the section "Infractions and Punishment," page 20, fouls are improper actions that are committed, 1. By one player upon another, 2. On the field of play, and, 3. While the ball is in play.

These same actions, committed by non-players; upon non-players; off the field of play; or while play is stopped are not technically fouls, but are treated as misconduct.

Any foul, if particularly blatant, may also be penalized as misconduct under the categories of "Ungentlemanly Conduct," "Violent Conduct," or "Serious Foul Play," in addition to punishment as a foul. In that case, a caution or ejection may be issued, in addition to the appropriate form of free-kick. See "Misconduct," page 53.

There are two classes of fouls: "major" and "minor."

The 9 Major-Fouls

The 9 major-fouls, or penal-fouls, are penalized by the awarding of **direct-free-kicks** to the fouled team. (Direct-free-kicks may score if the ball passes directly through the opposing team's goal.)

Major-fouls are particularly costly when players commit them within their own penalty-areas, for the opposing team is then awarded a special kick called a "penalty-kick." Because of severe restrictions placed on the defending team, a penalty-kick often results in a score. See "Penalty-Kicks," page 50.

With the exception of the "hand-ball" (see below), major-fouls are defined as committed against opponents only.

The nine major-fouls are:

1. **KICKING OR ATTEMPTING TO KICK AN OPPONENT:** This includes "going over the ball" and kicking an opponent's leg.

2. **TRIPPING AN OPPONENT:** Or, throwing an opponent with the legs, or stooping near an opponent in order to trip. This foul is often called after a failed attempt to "tackle," or challenge an opponent for control of the ball by blocking it with the feet. A botched tackle that brings an opponent to the ground, especially when attempted from behind, may result in a call for tripping.

3. **JUMPING AT AN OPPONENT:** Especially jumping at a goal-keeper who is already in the air.

4. **VIOLENT OR DANGEROUS CHARGING OF AN OPPONENT:** Charging with a swing of the arm or an intent to harm is penalized. However, even extremely vigorous charging that knocks a player to the ground is allowed as long as it is fair, and the intention is to play the ball, not the opponent. See "Some Basic Concepts," page 8.

5. **CHARGING AN OPPONENT FROM BEHIND:** This is not allowed, except for non-violent charging from behind when the opponent is intentionally turning his back and screening the ball. See following section, "Obstruction."

6. **STRIKING OR ATTEMPTING TO STRIKE AN OPPONENT:** Spitting is considered a form of striking. It is also "striking" to intentionally throw the ball or any other object at an opponent.

7. **HOLDING AN OPPONENT:** This includes grabbing an opponent or his uniform, or using an outstretched arm to entangle an opponent.

8. **PUSHING AN OPPONENT.**

9. **HANDLING, OR "HAND-BALL":** Only goal-keepers playing within their own penalty-areas or included goal-areas may handle the ball. However, any player is allowed completely accidental and passive contact with the ball, with absolutely no intention of playing it. An illegal attempt to handle the ball which fails to make contact is not called.

The Minor-Fouls

Minor-fouls are penalized by the awarding of **indirect-free-kicks** to the fouled team. As with major-fouls, minor-fouls may receive additional punishment as misconduct, if committed repeatedly, or if the violation is particularly blatant.

In practice, minor-fouls are usually called when committed against opponents. However, minor-fouls may be committed against any player, or even against oneself, in the case of "dangerous play."

The minor-fouls are:

1. **DANGEROUS PLAY:** This includes not only acts such as high kicking near an opponent's head, but also situations where players might put *themselves* into danger, *e.g.*, diving low to head a ball below waist level while other players are trying to kick it. Dangerous play may be called even if accidental.

2. **FAIR-CHARGING OFF THE BALL:** Fair-charging is only allowed while attempting to play the ball. Fair-charging is illegal if the main intention is to bump the other player, or if the ball is obviously not within playable range.

3. **OBSTRUCTION:** It is allowable to use the body to block an opponent's path to the ball, but only if the ball is in playable range, and the main intention is to play the ball. This is called "screening."

Obstruction is prohibited if the main intention is to block the other player, or if the ball is obviously not within playable range. Actual contact is not necessary for the call to be made. Arm waving, standing in an obstructing position, or threatening a collision may all be interpreted as obstruction if the primary intent is to block an opponent from playing the ball.

Obstructing the goal-keeper is also prohibited when the goal-keeper is attempting to release the ball back into play.

4. **CHARGING THE GOAL-KEEPER ILLEGALLY:** The goal-keepers are partially protected from charging within their own penalty-areas and the included goal-areas. See "The Goal-Keepers," page 16.

"Pseudo Minor-Fouls"

Included in this category are four types of violations not technically involving "fouls," but that are nevertheless treated in a similar fashion.

The following violations are penalized by the awarding of **indirect-free-kicks** to the opposing team:

1. **GOAL-KEEPER VIOLATIONS:** Goal-keepers are prohibited from taking more than four steps while holding the ball in their hands; time-wasting; double-possession; and "kicking-to-the-keeper." If the referee calls any of these prohibited maneuvers, the opposing team is awarded an indirect-free-kick. See "Goal-keeper Limitations," page 17.

2. **OFFSIDE VIOLATIONS:** With many exceptions, attacking players are generally prohibited from positioning themselves ahead of the ball. If a player is called offside, the opposing team is awarded an indirect-free-kick. See "The Offside-Rule," page 55.

3. **MISCONDUCT WHISTLES:** If the referee whistles the ball dead to issue a caution or ejection for an offense committed on the field of play, the game is restarted with an indirect-free-kick awarded to the opposing team, just as though a minor-foul had been committed. In cases where the misconduct included a major-foul, a direct-free-kick or penalty-kick is awarded instead. See "Misconduct," page 53.

4. **DOUBLE PLAY:** Generally, a player who puts the ball into play may not touch it again until it is touched by another player from either team. If he does, the opposing team is awarded an indirect-free-kick. For details, see individual sections on kick-offs, throw-ins, goal-kicks, corner-kicks, free-kicks and penalty-kicks.

Free-Kicks

The following rules apply to free-kicks, *i.e.*, **direct-free-kicks** and **indirect-free-kicks** awarded to the opposing team when a foul is committed. Direct-free-kicks are awarded to penalize the 9 major-fouls, and indirect-free-kicks are awarded to penalize the minor-fouls and "pseudo minor-fouls."

NOTE: There is one other type of kick awarded to penalize fouls. This is the "penalty-kick," which is covered in the following chapter. Penalty-kicks are awarded when a team commits one of the 9 major-fouls within its own penalty-area. The rules for penalty-kicks are very different from the rules for free-kicks. See "Penalty-Kicks," page 50.

General Rules For Free-Kicks

1. A **direct-free-kick** may score if the ball passes directly through the opposing team's goal, without being touched by any other player.

2. An **indirect-free-kick** may not score unless the ball is touched by a second player from either team after the initial kick.

3. Kicks are taken from the location of the offending player at the moment the foul is committed.

   Exception: A team taking a free-kick from its own goal-area may place the ball anywhere within the goal-area.

   Exception: Kicks may not be taken *against* a team from within its own goal-area. In that case, the ball is placed on the six-yard-line at the point nearest to where the foul occurred.

4. The referee will point briefly in the attacking direction of the team taking the kick. If necessary, the referee will also indicate where the ball is to be placed for the kick. Any member of the kicking team may place the ball on the ground, and any member may take the kick.

5. Defenders may not distract or interfere with the kicker. They must stay at least 10 yards from the ball until it is put into play. If a team is to take

To signal an indirect-free-kick, the referee will first point in the attacking direction of the team taking the kick...

Then, he will hold one hand up until the ball is kicked and touched by a second player, or until it goes out of play.

a free-kick from within its own penalty-area, opponents must also stay outside the penalty-area until the ball enters play.

Exception: If a kick is to be taken *against* a team from less than 10 yards of its own goal, they may form a "human wall" by standing on their own goal-line between the goal-posts. Their feet must remain on the goal-line until the ball is kicked.

6. The kicker's teammates may position themselves anywhere on the field, even within the defenders' "human wall." (They may not force their way in.)

7. The kick may be made at any time, even before the defenders have moved back the required 10 yards. This is called a "quick-free-kick."

8. The ball must be kicked while stationary on the ground.

9. The kick may be made in any direction.

10. The kick must be taken promptly. Minor feinting or "running over the ball" is usually tolerated, but undue time-wasting may be cautioned as ungentlemanly conduct.

11. The ball is in play when it has traveled one full revolution, about 28 inches.

    Exception: Kicks by a team from within its own penalty-area are not in play until they have also passed completely outside the penalty-area and onto the field of play.

12. The Offside-Rule *does* apply at the moment of the initial kick, *i.e.*, it is possible for the first player to touch the ball after the initial kick to be called offside. See "The Offside-Rule," page 55.

13. Once the ball is in play, the kicker is not allowed to contact it again until it has been touched by another player. This is double-play, punished by giving an indirect-free-kick to the opposing team.

14. A re-kick is taken if the ball fails to enter play legally.

15. Repeated procedural violations may be treated as misconduct if intentional.

For a direct-free-kick, the referee will point briefly in the attacking direction of the team taking the kick.

Penalty-Kicks

A penalty-kick is awarded to opponents when a team commits one of the 9 major-fouls inside its own penalty-area or the included goal-area.

A penalty-kick is a devastating call, because it often results in a goal being scored against the fouling team.

Only the goal-keeper is allowed to defend the penalty-kick.

1. The referee will whistle and point to the fouling team's penalty-kick-mark to indicate that he has called a major-foul within their penalty-area.

2. The ball is placed stationary on the fouling team's penalty-kick-mark (12 yards out from their goal). It must be placed exactly on the penalty-kick-mark, even if there is a hole or a muddy spot there.

3. All players except the kicker and the defending goal-keeper must remain outside the penalty-area, as well as outside the penalty-arc, until the ball is kicked.

4. The goal-keeper must stand stationary in the goal with his feet on the goal-line. He may shift his weight, but he may not make distracting gestures while waiting for the kick.

5. Any member of the attacking team may take the kick, including the attacking goal-keeper. The kicker must be identified to the referee.

6. The kicker must wait for a signal from the referee. He may make a running start, but feinting or running over the ball are prohibited, and the kick must be made in one continuous motion.

7. The kick is "direct." It may score if it passes directly through the defending goal, or if it passes through the goal after bouncing off the goal-keeper, the goal-posts, the cross-bar, or any combination.

8. The ball is in play when it has traveled forward one full revolution. It may then be kicked by any player except the player who took the original kick. A kick that fails to put the ball into play is retaken.

PENALTY-KICKS AT A GLANCE
What Happens If...? *

Ball enters goal, and...

DEFENDING TEAM ENCROACHES	KICKING TEAM ENCROACHES	NEITHER TEAM ENCROACHES	BOTH TEAMS ENCROACH	GOAL-KEEPER MOVEMENT	DOUBLE-PLAY
Goal Counted Caution Violator Defenders Kick-Off	Goal Not Counted Caution Violator Re-Kick	Goal Counted Defenders Kick-Off	Goal Not Counted Caution Violators Re-Kick	Goal Counted Defenders Kick-Off	Goal Not Counted Caution Violator Defenders Indirect-Free-Kick

Ball flies or bounces directly out-of-bounds over goal-line, and...

DEFENDING TEAM ENCROACHES	KICKING TEAM ENCROACHES	NEITHER TEAM ENCROACHES	BOTH TEAMS ENCROACH	GOAL-KEEPER MOVEMENT	DOUBLE-PLAY
Caution Violator Re-Kick	Caution Violator Defenders Goal-Kick	Defenders Goal-Kick	Caution Violators Re-Kick	Re-Kick	Caution Violator Defenders Indirect-Free-Kick

Goal-keeper deflects ball out-of-bounds over goal-line, and...

DEFENDING TEAM ENCROACHES	KICKING TEAM ENCROACHES	NEITHER TEAM ENCROACHES	BOTH TEAMS ENCROACH	GOAL-KEEPER MOVEMENT	DOUBLE-PLAY
Caution Violator Re-Kick	Caution Violator Attackers Corner-Kick	Attackers Corner-Kick	Caution Violators Re-Kick	Re-Kick	Caution Violator Defenders Indirect-Free-Kick

Goal-keeper saves ball, and...

DEFENDING TEAM ENCROACHES	KICKING TEAM ENCROACHES	NEITHER TEAM ENCROACHES	BOTH TEAMS ENCROACH	GOAL-KEEPER MOVEMENT	DOUBLE-PLAY
Caution Violator Re-Kick	Caution Violator Defenders Indirect-Free-Kick	Goalie Releases Into Play	Caution Violators Re-Kick	Re-Kick	Caution Violator Defenders Indirect-Free-Kick

Ball rebounds onto field, or enters play, and...

DEFENDING TEAM ENCROACHES	KICKING TEAM ENCROACHES	NEITHER TEAM ENCROACHES	BOTH TEAMS ENCROACH	GOAL-KEEPER MOVEMENT	DOUBLE-PLAY
Caution Violator Re-Kick	Caution Violator Defenders Indirect-Free-Kick	Play On!	Caution Violators Re-Kick	Re-Kick	Caution Violator Defenders Indirect-Free-Kick

* The referee will not stop play if he sees a violation during the taking of a penalty-kick. He will first allow the kick to proceed, and he will observe the results before deciding the proper course of action.

9. The kicker may not touch the ball again until it has been touched by another player from either team. This is double-play, punished by giving an indirect-free-kick to the opposing team.

10. The Offside-Rule applies at the moment the ball is kicked. Offside may be called if the ball is kicked to a teammate in an offside position, or if the ball rebounds off the goal to a teammate in an offside position.

11. If *defenders* encroach or violate procedures: 1. Successful shots are allowed to stand; or, 2. Missed shots are re-taken.

12. If *attackers* encroach or violate procedures: 1. Successful shots must be re-taken; or, 2. Missed shots are allowed to stand, with the ball being given over to the defending team.

    When a missed shot is allowed to stand, the defending team will put the ball back into play using one of two methods, depending on the exact circumstances:

    a. If the ball goes untouched out-of-bounds, they get a goal-kick.

    b. If the ball rebounds onto the field, the referee will whistle it dead, caution the offending attacker, and give an indirect-free-kick to the defenders.

    Exception: If attackers encroach and the shot misses because the goal-keeper deflects it out-of-bounds, the missed shot stands, but the *attacking team* gets the ball back and puts it into play with a corner-kick. (Opponents of the team that last touched it.)

13. If *both attackers and defenders* encroach or violate procedures, the kick is retaken, regardless of the outcome.

14. If *neither team* encroaches or violates, and the goal-keeper deflects the ball out-of-bounds over the goal-line, the attacking team gets it, and puts it back into play with a corner-kick.

15. If *neither team* violates, and the kick misses completely or deflects off the goal and goes out-of-bounds over the goal-line, the defending team is awarded the ball and puts it back into play with a goal-kick.

16. If an outside agent touches the shot before it goes into the goal, the kick is retaken. If the ball has already bounced off the goal when interfered with, a drop-ball is taken.

17. If the goal-keeper saves the ball, play continues, and he releases it back into play.

18. A game or period may not end while either team is entitled to take a penalty-kick. If a foul justifying a penalty-kick occurs just as time runs out, the referee will extend time to allow the kick to be taken or retaken. During a penalty-kick taken in extended time, no players are allowed to participate except the kicker and the defending goal-keeper. The game or period ends at the moment the kick has been taken or retaken, and the referee has decided whether or not a goal has been scored.

19. A caution is issued for all violations of penalty-kick procedures except for goal-keeper movement.

Misconduct

As explained in the section, "Infractions and Punishment," page 20, misconduct violations involve actions against the spirit of the game, such as time-wasting, arguing with the referee, or ungentlemanly conduct.

Also treated as misconduct are actions that would otherwise be considered "fouls," but that have been committed while the ball is not in play; against persons other than players (officials, spectators, etc.); or by substitutes on the bench. Finally, punishment for misconduct may be added to the penalty for any foul which is flagrant or uses excessive force.

Any misconduct committed on the field for which the referee blows his whistle to stop play may be considered a "pseudo-minor-foul," since play is restarted with an indirect-free-kick awarded to the offended team.

As in the case of fouls, there are two classes of misconduct violations, "major" and "minor":

The referee will display a "yellow-card" for a caution, and a "red-card" for an ejection.

The Major-Misconduct Violations

The major misconduct violations result in an immediate **ejection (red-card)** from the game. Players ejected during the game (or at half-time) may not be replaced. Their teams must play on shorthanded.

1. **VIOLENT CONDUCT:** Includes physical attacks while not playing the ball, *i.e.,* off the ball during play, while play is stopped, or against someone other than an opponent.

2. **SERIOUS FOUL PLAY:** There are two types of serious foul play. One type includes particularly violent fouling against an opponent during a play for the ball. The second type of serious foul play is the "professional foul" against the spirit of the game, *i.e.,* any deliberate foul committed to neutralize an obvious scoring opportunity. Deliberate tripping to stop a shot, or a deliberate handball to stop a shot would fall into this category.

3. **FOUL OR ABUSIVE LANGUAGE:** Includes comments from the side-line. This category provides a basis for ejection when the abusive language goes beyond "ungentlemanly conduct," a minor-misconduct violation. See following section.

4. **RECEIPT OF A SECOND CAUTION FOR ANY REASON:** If a player who has already received a caution commits any second cautionable offense, an ejection (red-card) is issued. The referee will first briefly display the yellow-card, and then immediately display the red-card to indicate that an ejection has resulted from a second cautionable infraction.

The Minor Misconduct Violations

For minor-misconduct, the referee will issue a formal **caution (yellow-card)**. As noted previously, any second cautionable offense will result in ejection. The minor misconduct violations:

1. **UNAUTHORIZED SUBSTITUTION OR ENTRY/EXIT:** Temporarily going out-of-bounds is allowed during throw-ins, corner-kicks, when lining up for free-kicks, or when trying to play the ball near the edge of the field. With a single exception, all other entries or exits from the field may be made only with the permission of the referee. The exception? A player may step off the field temporarily in order to avoid being called offside. See "The Offside Rule," page 55.

2. **PERSISTENT RULE BREAKING:** Repeated fouling or breaking of the rules may result in a caution being issued, in addition to whatever other penalty may be justified. This also applies to the player who repeatedly commits fouls with the knowledge that the referee will probably invoke the Advantage-Clause, and not award a free-kick to the opposing team.

3. **ARGUING WITH THE REFEREE (DISSENT):** Verbal arguing, gesturing or other actions showing dissent from the referee's decisions are not allowed, even if they are not aimed directly at the referee. Youth leagues may allow players to request clarification of calls by the referee.

4. **UNGENTLEMANLY CONDUCT:** A catch-all category that includes any action not in the spirit of the game. Includes hollering, mocking, contempt, time-wasting, gesturing, distracting, throwing or kicking the ball away, or any other conduct deemed inappropriate by the referee. This category also includes *any action* during the game that, in the opinion of the referee, may give an unfair advantage to either team.

5. **PROCEDURAL VIOLATIONS:** Encroachment or intentional failure to put the ball into play properly may result in cautions, or even ejections if repeated. In the special case of penalty-kicks, *all* procedural violations except for goal-keeper movement result in a caution for the offender.

The Offside-Rule

The basic idea of the Offside-Rule is that attacking players may not position themselves ahead of the ball.

The purpose of the rule is identical to the "Three Second Rule" in basketball; it is designed to prevent attacking players from hanging around the mouth of the goal waiting for a pass and an easy score.

Offside may be considered a "pseudo minor-foul," since it results in an indirect-free-kick for the defending team. The kick is taken from the position of the offside attacker at the instant the offside violation occurred.

WHEN CALLED: There are two basic requirements that must be *satisfied simultaneously* in order to call an attacking player offside:

1. The attacker must be ahead of the ball. (Note: It's okay to be *even* with the ball. To be called offside, the attacker must actually be between the ball and the defending team's goal-line).

2. The attacker must somehow be actively involved in the game at the exact instant the ball is played or shot by a teammate.

OFFSIDE: The Basic Violation

THE BASIC OFFSIDE VIOLATION:

- **Attacker 1 passes the ball to teammate, Attacker 2.**

- **Attacker 2 is ahead of the ball at the moment it is kicked.**

- **Attacker 2 receives ball & scores.**

- **Attacker 2 is called offside.**

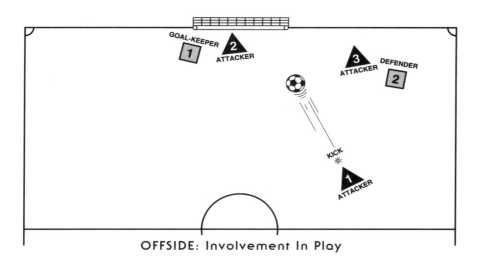

OFFSIDE: Involvement In Play

- **Attacker 1 shoots on goal.**

- **Attackers 2 & 3 are positioned ahead of the ball.**

- **Attackers 2 & 3 prevent defenders from stopping the shot.**

- **Attackers 2 & 3 are "involved in play."**

- **Attackers 2 & 3 are called offside.**

Interpretation of the requirement for active involvement is quite broad. Offside will be called if the attacker who is in an offside position is distracting, obstructing, blocking vision, moving to receive a pass, or attempting to play the ball before a defender can get to it.

Mere involvement in the game is what counts. It is not necessary that the ball actually be played to the offside player.

"AT THE MOMENT…": An important factor in making the offside call is the phrase "at the moment the ball is played." Regardless of what may happen before or after, the call is made if, and only if, the player is offside at that crucial moment. There are two important consequences of this rule:

1. It is entirely legal to pass the ball to an empty part of the field that may be an offside position. A teammate may then run up to the ball and play it. As long as the teammate himself was not offside at the *moment the ball was passed*, no offside is called.

2. Conversely, an offside player may not avoid the call by running back to a legal position after the ball is kicked. If he was offside *at the moment of the kick*, the call is made.

IMPORTANT EXEMPTIONS: There are many situations in which the Offside-Rule *does not apply*:

1. Offside is not called if there are at least two defenders between the attacker and the defending goal-line. This can be the goal-keeper plus one other defender. For the purpose of calling offside, a defender who is even with an attacker is considered to be between him and the goal.

2. Offside is not called at the defensive end of the field. If an attacking player is on his own team's side of the halfway-line, offside does not apply to him.

3. Offside is not called if the attacker is *completely* uninvolved in play.

4. Offside is not called if the ball was last played by an opponent. A ball that rebounds passively off an opponent is not considered to have been "played" by him. If the kick that caused the rebound was made by a teammate of the offside player, the call will be made.

5. Offside is not called if the ball is received as a direct result of a corner-kick, goal-kick, throw-in, or during the initial drop of a drop-ball. It does apply, however, during direct- or indirect-free-kicks, penalty-kicks, and during a goal-keeper clearing kick or throw.

6. Offside is not called if the attacking player is merely even with the ball. For offside to apply, the attacker must actually be ahead of the ball.

7. Offside is not called if the offside player runs off the field before the ball is played, and he is not interfering with opponents. (This is an exception to the rule that players may leave the field only when they have permission from the referee.) The player may not return until his team loses the ball, or until a natural stoppage of play occurs.

8. Offside is not called if an attacker is put into an offside position by a defender who intentionally runs off the field, thus leaving fewer than two defenders between the attacker and the defending goal-line.

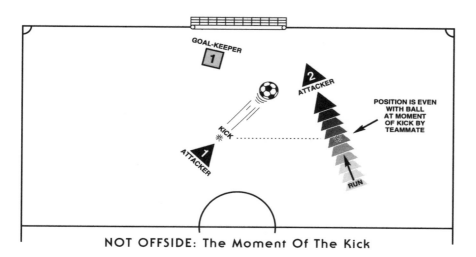

NOT OFFSIDE: The Moment Of The Kick

NOT OFFSIDE!
(AT THE MOMENT OF THE KICK)

- Attacker 1 makes a forward pass into an empty part of the field that is in an offside position.

- Attacker 2 runs forward and gets the ball.

- However, at the moment of the kick, Attacker 2 was even with the ball, and therefore not in an offside position.

- Attacker 2 is not called offside.

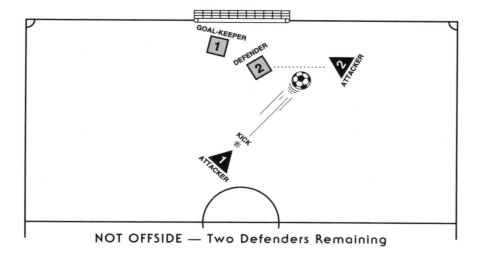

NOT OFFSIDE — Two Defenders Remaining

NOT OFFSIDE!
(TWO DEFENDERS REMAINING)

- Attacker 1 passes ball forward to teammate, Attacker 2.

- There are two defenders between Attacker 2 and the goal-line.

- Attacker 2 is not called offside.

- Note: Defender 2 is merely *even* with Attacker 2, not ahead of him.

For the purpose of calling offside, a defender who is even with an attacker is considered to be between the attacker and the goal-line.

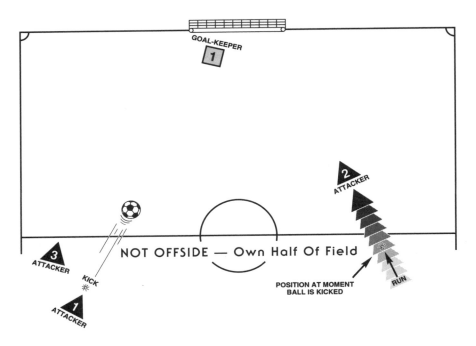

NOT OFFSIDE — Own Half Of Field

NOT OFFSIDE!
(OWN HALF OF FIELD)

- Attacker 1 passes ball across the half-way line.

- Attackers 2 & 3 are ahead of the ball, and have only one defender between them and the goal-line.

- But, Attackers 2 & 3 are on their own half of the field at the moment of the kick.

- After the kick, Attacker 2 crosses the halfway-line to get the ball.

- Neither Attacker 2 nor Attacker 3 is called offside, because both were on their own half of the field at the moment of the kick.

NOT OFFSIDE — Not Involved In Play

NOT OFFSIDE!
(NOT INVOLVED IN PLAY)

- Attacker 1 shoots on goal.

- Attacker 2 is ahead of the ball, and there is only one defender between him and the goal-line.

- However, Attacker 2 is completely uninvolved in play.

- Attacker 2 is not called offside.

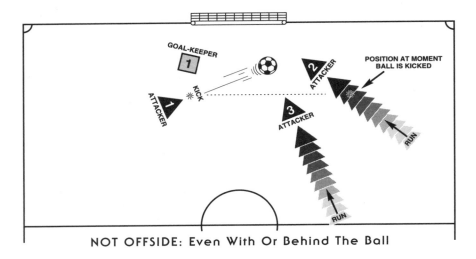

NOT OFFSIDE: Even With Or Behind The Ball

NOT OFFSIDE!
(EVEN WITH OR BEHIND THE BALL)

- Attacker 1 passes the ball to a position directly in front of the goal.

- There is only one defender left.

- Attackers 2 & 3 close in to take the shot.

- Neither Attacker 2 nor Attacker 3 is called offside, because they were both even with the ball or behind it at the moment the ball was played.

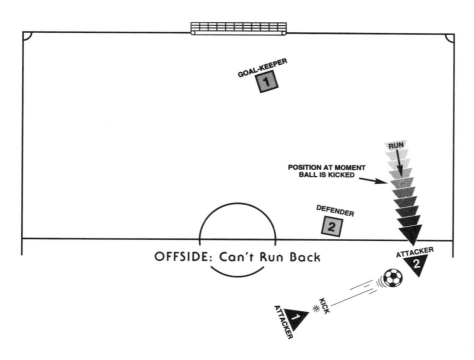

OFFSIDE: Can't Run Back

OFFSIDE!
(CAN'T RUN BACK)

- Attacker 1 passes the ball toward teammate, Attacker 2.

- Attacker 2 realizes he is offside.

- As the ball rolls towards him, he runs back across the halfway-line.

- Attacker 2 is now not in an offside position, because he is on his own half of the field. Further, he now has two defenders between him and the goal-line.

- However, Attacker 2 *was* in an offside position at the moment the ball was played to him.

- Attacker 2 is called offside.

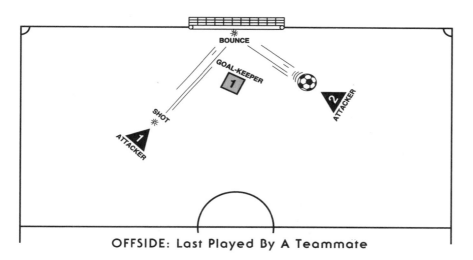

OFFSIDE: Last Played By A Teammate

OFFSIDE!
(LAST PLAYED BY A TEAMMATE)

- Attacker 1 shoots on goal.

- At that moment, Attacker 2 is in an offside position, but is not involved in the play.

- However, the ball bounces passively off the cross-bar to Attacker 2, who scores.

- Attacker 2 is now involved in play, and he was in an offside position at the moment the ball was last played by a teammate.

- Attacker 2 is called offside.

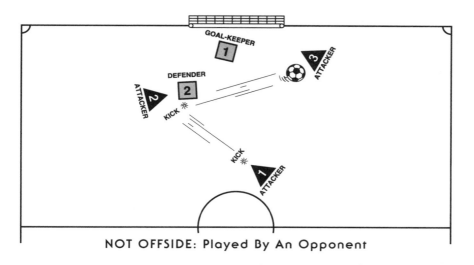

NOT OFFSIDE: Played By An Opponent

NOT OFFSIDE!
(PLAYED BY AN OPPONENT)

- Attacker 1 passes toward teammate, Attacker 2.

- Attacker 3 is in an offside position, but is uninvolved in play.

- Defender 2 *actively* kicks the ball, but it goes to Attacker 3, who scores.

- Attacker 3 is not called offside, because the ball was last played by an opponent.

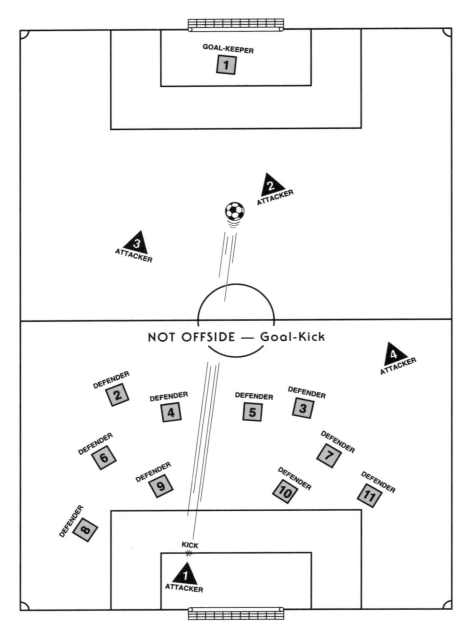

GOAL-KEEPER
1

2 ATTACKER

3 ATTACKER

NOT OFFSIDE — Goal-Kick

4 ATTACKER

DEFENDER **2**

DEFENDER **4**

DEFENDER **5**

DEFENDER **3**

DEFENDER **6**

DEFENDER **7**

DEFENDER **9**

DEFENDER **10**

DEFENDER **11**

DEFENDER **8**

KICK

1 ATTACKER

NOT OFFSIDE! (GOAL-KICK)

- The attacking team is awarded a goal-kick, and Attackers 2 & 3 position themselves far down field, behind all defenders except the goal-keeper.

- The kick flies over the heads of all defenders to Attacker 2, who collects the ball and scores.

- Attacker 2 is ahead of the ball, in the defenders' end of the field, involved in play, and has only one defender between him and the goal-line!

- However, Attacker 2 is not called offside, because The Offside-Rule does not apply during a goal-kick.

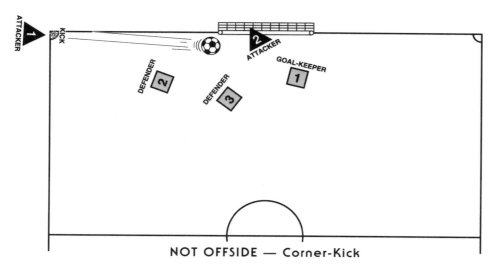

NOT OFFSIDE — Corner-Kick

NOT OFFSIDE!
(CORNER-KICK)

- During a corner-kick, Attacker 2 positions himself behind all defenders, even the goal-keeper.

- The ball goes directly to Attacker 2, who scores easily.

- Attacker 2 is not called offside, because he received the ball directly from a corner-kick.

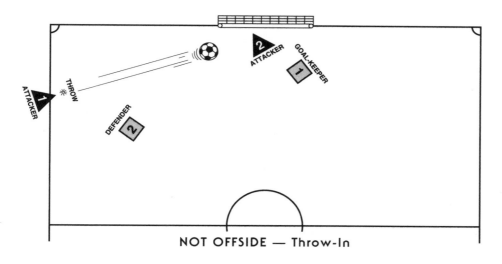

NOT OFFSIDE — Throw-In

NOT OFFSIDE!
(THROW-IN)

- During a throw-in, Attacker 2 positions himself behind all defenders, even the goal-keeper.

- The ball goes directly to Attacker 2, who scores easily.

- Attacker 2 is not called offside, because he received the ball directly from a throw-in.

NOT OFFSIDE: Drop-Ball

NOT OFFSIDE!
(DROP-BALL)

- The referee calls a drop-ball, and Attacker 1 positions himself behind all defenders except the goal-keeper.

- The ball bounces untouched directly to Attacker 1, who collects it and scores.

- Attacker 1 is not called offside, because he received the ball directly from a drop-ball.

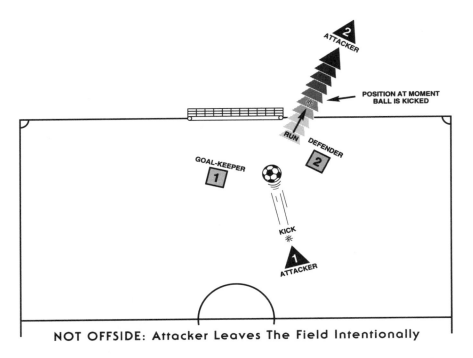

NOT OFFSIDE: Attacker Leaves The Field Intentionally

NOT OFFSIDE!
(ATTACKER LEAVES THE FIELD INTENTIONALLY)

- Attacker 1 prepares to shoot on goal.

- Attacker 2 sees he will be caught in an offside position. He is ahead of all defenders, and may be called for interfering with Defender 2.

- Attacker 2 anticipates the shot, and runs off the field just before the ball is kicked.

- At the moment of the shot, Attacker 2 is outside the goal-line.

- Attacker 2 is not called offside, because it is legal to leave the field temporarily in this situation.

- Attacker 2 may not re-enter the field until his team loses the ball, or until a natural stoppage of play occurs.

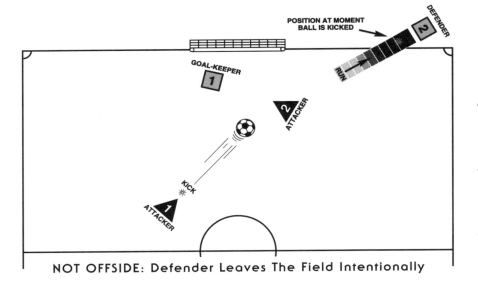

NOT OFFSIDE: Defender Leaves The Field Intentionally

NOT OFFSIDE!
(DEFENDER LEAVES THE FIELD INTENTIONALLY)

- Attacker 1 prepares to pass the ball to Attacker 2, who is in a legal position, with two defenders between him and the goal-line.

- Defender 2 anticipates the pass, and quickly runs off the field, leaving Attacker 2 in an offside position at the moment of the kick.

- Attacker 2 is not called offside, because he was put in an offside position by a defender intentionally leaving the field.

- Further, Defender 2 may be cautioned for leaving the field without the referee's permission.

Substitutions

In a regulation game, a team may have up to 5 substitutes on the sidelines. During the game, only 2 substitutions are allowed, and any player who is substituted for may not return.

Many leagues have more liberal rules regarding substitutions. In youth leagues, for example, an unlimited number of substitutions may be allowed, and players may be allowed to return to the field after they have been substituted for. See following section, "Youth League Substitutions."

The following rules apply to substitutions in regulation FIFA matches:

1. **INJURED PLAYERS:** Injured players may be substituted for, but only up to the limit of substitutions allowed. If an injury occurs after the maximum number of substitutions has been made, the team must play on shorthanded. However, injured players who have not been substituted for may return to the game.

2. **EJECTED PLAYERS:** Substitutions are not allowed for players ejected after the opening kick-off. An ejection during the game or at half-time means that the team must play shorthanded. However, players ejected before the game starts may be replaced. Substitutes ejected while waiting on the bench may not play.

3. **REFEREE PERMISSION:** All substitutions must be made upon a signal from the referee, and substitutes must enter the field at the halfway-line. They may not enter until the player they are replacing has left the field.

4. **WHEN ALLOWED:** Normally, substitutions are allowed only when play has been stopped for a throw-in, free-kick, etc. However, injured players re-entering the field may do so "on the fly" whenever the referee signals to them.

5. **GOAL-KEEPER SWITCHING:** If a player on the field wishes to switch places with the goal-keeper, the referee must be notified in advance, and a special goal-keeper shirt must be worn by the new goal-keeper. The goal-keeper may not be switched "on the fly."

The linesman's signal to the referee that one of the teams wishes to make a substitution. The referee will allow the substitution at the next natural stoppage of play.

6. **PENALTIES FOR SUBSTITUTION VIOLATIONS:** If a substitute enters the field without permission, play is stopped, a caution is issued, the player is removed, and play is resumed with a drop-ball taken at the location of the ball at the time of the whistle.

The referee will not stop play for a goal-keeper switching violation, but will caution the players involved at the next natural stoppage of play.

Youth League Substitutions

Generally, youth leagues have more liberal rules for substitutions. Most youth leagues allow virtually unlimited substitutions, and also the return to the game of players who have been substituted for. However, the referee's permission is still required for all substitutions. Typically, substitutions may be made at the following times in youth league games:

1. **PRIOR TO A THROW-IN:** By the team in possession.

2. **PRIOR TO A GOAL-KICK:** Both teams may substitute.

3. **AFTER A GOAL HAS BEEN SCORED:** Both teams may substitute.

4. **DURING AN INJURY STOPPAGE:** Both teams may substitute.

5. **AT HALFTIME:** Both teams may substitute.

6. **AFTER A CAUTION:** The cautioned player may be substituted for.

Deciding The Winner Of The Game

The winner of the game is the team that has scored the most goals at the end of the final regular period of play.

In drawn games, the tied result may be allowed to stand, as is, or a winner may be decided through several methods including overtime periods, the taking of kicks from the penalty-kick-mark, a shoot-out, the drawing of lots, the flipping of a coin, or by league declaration.

Overtime Periods

If used, overtime play is usually divided into two, 15-minute halves with a 5-minute break in between. There is also usually a 5-minute break between the end of the regular game and the beginning of overtime play.

The team having the most goals at the end of the final overtime period is declared the winner.

Some leagues may specify shorter overtime periods, a single overtime period, or sudden-death overtime periods.

To begin overtime play, a coin-toss is used to determine which team will kick off, just as at the beginning of the game. The rules governing play during overtime periods are the same as for regular play.

Kicks Taken From The Penalty-Kick-Mark

To decide a winner by taking kicks from the penalty-kick-mark, the teams take what amount to alternating penalty-kicks until one team has scored more goals than the other.

The alternating kicks are taken in two stages.

First, a best-of-five series is kicked. Each team is given five alternating kicks, and the team that scores the most goals wins. If at any point in the series, either team falls so far behind that it becomes impossible for it to win or tie, then the opposing team is declared the winner.

If the teams are still tied after the best-of-five series, then they will kick a series of one-kick contests. Each team is given one kick for each round of the series. A winner is declared at the end of any round in which one team has scored and the other has not. If both teams miss, or if both teams score, another round is kicked. This process is continued until a winner is determined.

1. To begin the tie-breaking procedure, the referee will choose which goal will be used, and he will flip a coin. The winning team must shoot first.

2. All members of both teams who were playing at the end of the last regular period or the last overtime period must take kicks. This includes the two goal-keepers. If required players fail to show up for the taking of kicks, it cannot take place.

3. The basic procedures of penalty-kicks are followed, with the ball placed on the penalty-kick-mark and the defending goal-keeper required to stand stationary with his feet on the goal-line until the ball is kicked.

4. The goal-keeper of the kicking team (who will be needed to defend for the next kick) is allowed to stand just outside the penalty-area and penalty-arc, and may be no closer than 18 yards to the goal-line.

5. All other players must remain inside the center-circle until they are needed to take a kick. Then they must immediately return to the center-circle. No other persons are allowed on the field.

6. A goal-keeper who is injured during the taking of kicks may be substituted for from the bench, but only if his team has not already used its maximum allowed number of substitutions. Teammates on the field may also switch places with the goal-keeper, if desired. Otherwise, substitutions are not allowed.

7. Each player must kick, and no player may kick again until all of his teammates have kicked. However, no special order is required, and the order of kickers may be changed for each round. The referee will keep a careful record of the kicks.

Shoot-Outs

The concept of the shoot-out is similar to the taking of kicks from the penalty-kick-mark, with the major exception that the ball is placed 35 yards from the goal, and the kicker is given 5 seconds to put the ball into play, dribble, maneuver and score.

The shoot-out is typically a best-of-five series of one-on-one matches between the kickers and the goal-keepers:

1. The goal-keeper must wait on the goal-line until the whistle.

2. The kicker may dribble and take only a single shot during his allocated five seconds.

3. Neither player may foul, and the basic rules that apply to regular play are followed.

Drawing Lots Or Flipping A Coin

These methods may be used to determine a winner at the end of a regular game, after an overtime period has been played without a winner, or in case darkness or other factors stop an overtime period, the taking of kicks from the penalty-kick-mark, or a shoot-out already in progress.

League Declaration

If the game is abandoned without a winner for any reason, the league will decide if the game should be replayed, or if a winner should be declared. Some reasons a game might be abandoned include: Loss of order, poor weather or field conditions, equipment failure, insufficient players to continue, officials unable to continue, and interference from outside agents.

Glossary

ACCIDENTAL-FOUL: A foul committed unintentionally. Usually not penalized. See **Intentional-Foul, Deliberate-Foul**.

ADVANCING-FROM-THE-GOAL, NARROWING-THE-ANGLE: The movement of a defender towards an attacking player in order to reduce the area of the goal exposed to a possible shot. Usually applied to the goal-keeper.

ADVANTAGE-CLAUSE: The option of the referee to ignore a foul, if he feels that the fouled team will thus have a greater advantage.

ATTACK, OFFENSE: The team having possession of the ball, either during regular play, or while putting the ball into play with a kick-off, corner-kick, free-kick, etc. See **Defense**.

ATTACKING END OF THE FIELD: The end of the field opposite a team's own goal. See **Defensive End Of The Field**.

BACK-OF-DEFENSE: The area of the field between the defending goal-keeper and his nearest teammate.

BACKSPIN: A rearwards spin applied to the ball which causes it to stop quickly upon landing.

BACK-UP: See **Cover**.

BALANCE-IN-DEFENSE: A strategy that deploys defenders nearest to the ball in marking-man-to-man, while players away from the ball play zone defense. See **Marking, Zone-Defense**.

BASEBALL-THROW: A one-handed throw by the goal-keeper. See **Throw**.

BENDING-THE-BALL: Making a ball travel in a curving path by applying a side spin as it is kicked. See **Inswinger-Ball, Outswinger-Ball**.

BICYCLE-KICK, HITCH-KICK, OVERHEAD-VOLLEY, SCISSORS-KICK: An acrobatic kick made by leaping high into the air and kicking the ball with the body in a horizontal position.

BLIND-SIDE-RUN: The movement of an attacking player without the ball to a position outside of his opponents' field of view.

BLOCK-TACKLE: A tackle made by using the inside of the foot to block the ball against the foot of an opponent. See **Tackle**.

BOOKING: The referee's recording of a caution or ejection issued to a player.

BOXING, FISTING, PUNCHING: The deflection of a shot on goal by the goal-keeper using a one-handed or two-handed punching motion with the fists closed.

BREAKAWAY: A sudden attack that leaves defenders behind.

BRIDGING: Illegally bending over or stooping near an opponent, causing the opponent to lose balance.

CAUTION, YELLOW-CARD: A formal notification that a misconduct infraction has been recorded. The referee will display a yellow-card to signify that an official caution has been issued. If a player receives two yellow-cards, he is ejected from the game. See **Ejection, Misconduct**.

CENTER-CIRCLE: A circle of 10 yards radius in the center of the field. Opponents of the kicking team must remain outside this circle during kick-offs.

CENTER-FORWARDS: Forwards stationed near the center line of the field. See **Forwards**.

CENTER-HALFBACKS: Halfbacks stationed near the center line of the field. See **Halfbacks**.

CENTERING, CENTER-PASSING, "CENTER IT!": To pass the ball from the sidelines of the field to an area in front of a goal. Used to create scoring opportunities.

CENTER LINE: An unmarked, imaginary line running lengthwise down the middle of the field from one goal to the other. See **Halfway-Line**.

CENTER-MARK, CENTER-SPOT: A marked point in the exact center of the field. Kick-offs are made from this point.

CENTER-SPOT: See **Center-Mark**.

CHARGING: See **Fair-Charging**.

CHARGING-FROM-BEHIND: Intentionally contacting an opponent arm-to-arm from the rear. A major-foul unless the opponent is screening the ball. See **Fair-Charging, Screening**.

CHEST-TRAPPING, CHESTING: See **Receiving**.

CHIP-PASS: A short, high-flying pass often made with backspin by kicking the lower part of the ball. See **Pass**.

CLEAR, CLEARING THROW, CLEARING KICK: A long kick or throw away from the defensive goal that neutralizes a scoring threat. Often by the goal-keeper.

CLUB-LINESMEN: Volunteer assistants to the referee supplied by the clubs competing in a match. They assist in signalling out-of-bounds. See **Linesmen, Neutral-Linesmen**.

COACHING-AREAS: Special areas just outside the touch-lines and near the benches. Coaches may convey tactical instructions to their teams in a reasonable manner from these areas.

COIN-TOSS: The method of deciding which team will take a kick-off.

COLLECTING: See **Receiving**.

CONCENTRATION-OF-DEFENSE: The clustering of defenders in a particular area of the field, especially near the goal area.

CORNER-AREAS, QUARTER-CIRCLES: The quarter-circles located in the four corners of the field. They have a radius of three feet, and corner-kicks are taken from them.

CORNER-FLAGS: Flags marking the corners of the field.

Corner-Kick: A kick by the attacking team to put the ball back into play after the defending team has driven it out-of-bounds over its own goal-line. See **Goal-Kick**.

Cover, Back-Up: Defensive players positioning themselves behind a team member who is challenging an attacker for the ball. See **Support**.

Cross, Cross-Pass: A pass made transversely across the field.

Cross-Bar: The horizontal bar eight feet off the ground that connects the goal-posts.

Dangerous-Play: Play that risks injury. Includes putting oneself into danger. A minor-foul.

Dead-Ball: A temporary suspension of play caused by the ball passing out-of-bounds, or by the referee whistling the ball dead.

Decoy-Run: A deceptive moment into a threatening field position. Intended to create playing space for a teammate.

Defense: The team not having possession of the ball. See **Attack**.

Defensive End Of The Field: The end of the field containing a team's own goal. See **Attacking End Of The Field**.

Deliberate-Foul: A foul committed with the main intent being to commit the foul, not play the ball. May draw a caution or ejection in addition to a free-kick. See **Accidental-Foul**, **Intentional-Foul**.

Diagonal-Cross: A pass made forward and diagonally across the field.

Diagonal-System: A system of officiating games wherein the referee runs back and forth along an imaginary line that goes diagonally from one corner of the field to the other.

Direct-Free-Kick: A free-kick that may score if it goes directly into the opponent's goal. See **Free-Kick**, **Indirect-Free-Kick**.

Distribution, Release: A kick or throw by the goal-keeper to put the ball into play after he has caught it.

Double-Play: After putting the ball into play, a player may not touch the ball again until it has been touched by another player from either team. Double-play is prohibited during kick-offs, free-kicks, penalty-kicks, goal-kicks, corner-kicks, and throw-ins.

Double-Possession: An illegal second possession of the ball by a goal-keeper after he has released it into play.

Dribble: To move the ball along with a series of short running kicks.

Drive: To move the ball with a series of long kicks and following runs.

Drop-Ball: A method of restarting play in which the referee drops the ball to the ground between opposing players.

Dummy: To fake the receipt of a pass, and let it go by to a teammate instead.

Eighteen-Yard-Lines: The lines that mark the edges of the penalty-areas nearest the middle of the field. These lines are eighteen yards from the goal-lines.

Ejection, Send-Off: A formal ejection of a player or other person from a match. The referee will display a red-card to signify that the offender has been officially ejected from the game. See **Caution**.

Encroachment: The illegal movement of a defender to within a prohibited distance from the kicker during kick-offs, free-kicks, penalty-kicks, goal-kicks, and corner-kicks.

End-Lines: See **Goal-Lines**.

ENGLISH: See **Spin**.

FAIR-CHARGING, CHARGING, SHOULDER-CHARGING: Legal physical shoulder contact with an opponent when the ball is within playing range. The intention must be to play the ball, not the opponent, and contact may only be made on the sides of the shoulders, not on the chest or spine. The contact must be non-violent.

FAR-POST: Whichever goal-post is farthest from the ball at any particular moment of play. See **Near-Post**.

FAR-POST-CROSS: A pass made toward the goal-post farthest from the kicker. See **Near-Post-Cross**.

FÉDÉRATION INTERNATIONALE DE FOOTBALL ASSOCIATION (FIFA), (FEE'-FAH): The worldwide governing body for soccer, located in Zurich, Switzerland.

FEINT: To fake any move, such as a pass or a kick.

FIELD-OF-PLAY, PITCH: The rectangular playing field, which measures 100-130 yards long, by 50-100 yards wide. The goals, boundary-lines and corner-flags are considered part of the field.

FIFA: See **Fédération Internationale de Football Association**.

FISTING: See **Boxing**.

FLANKS: The areas of the playing field nearest the sidelines.

FLICK-PASS: A sideways pass made with the outside of the foot.

FOOT-TRAPPING: See **Receiving**.

FORMATIONS: The strategic positioning of the players, which assigns them their primary duties and areas of responsibility. The goal-keeper plays nearest the goal. Next come the fullbacks. Then the halfbacks. Finally, the forwards are positioned closest to the opponents' goal. Formations are identified by listing the number of players in each position, counting outwards from the goal. The goal-keeper is not counted. Thus, an attack-oriented 2-4-4 formation would have two fullbacks, four halfbacks and four forwards. Other formations include the balanced 4-3-3, and the defense-oriented 4-4-2. See illustration, page 19.

FORWARDS, STRIKERS: Attacking players stationed at the front of a team's formation. See **Formation**.

FOULS: Improper action intentionally inflicted upon another player during play. Also includes the "hand-ball" and "dangerous play." Fouls are punished by the awarding of free-kicks to the fouled team.

FOUR-STEP-RULE: After gaining hand possession of the ball, the goal-keeper may take a maximum of four steps before releasing it back into play.

FREE-KICK: A kick awarded to penalize a foul. The ball is placed on the ground, and then it is kicked by a member of the fouled team without interference from defenders. See **Direct-Free-Kick** and **Indirect-Free-Kick**.

FULLBACKS: Defensive players stationed at the rear of a team's formation between the goal-keeper and the halfbacks. See **Formation**.

FULL-VOLLEY: See **Volley**.

GIVE-AND-GO-PASS, ONE-TWO-PASS: A combination pass made by kicking the ball to a teammate who immediately returns it.

GOAL: The rectangular frameworks at each end of the field through which the ball is kicked. Also, the point that is scored when the ball is driven through one of the goals.

GOAL-AREAS: the marked, rectangular 6 by 20-yard areas directly in front of the goals.

GOALIE: See **Goal-Keeper**.

GOAL-KEEPER, KEEPER, GOALIE: A defensive player assigned to guard his team's goal. The goal-keeper is the only player allowed to touch the ball with the hands.

GOAL-KICK: A kick by the defending team to put the ball back into play after it has been driven out-of-bounds over their goal-line by the attacking team. See **Corner-Kick**.

GOAL-LINES, END-LINES: The marked lines, 50-100 yards long, that define the ends of the field.

GOAL-NETS: Open mesh nets attached across the backs of the goals.

GOAL-POSTS: The pairs of eight-foot-high vertical posts marking the goals at each end of the field.

GOAL-SIDE, GOAL-SIDE-OF-THE-BALL, GOAL-SIDE-POSITION: The defensive player's position, between the ball or an opponent and his own goal.

GOING-OVER-THE-BALL, OVER-THE-BALL: Playing the foot over or near a ball so that an opponent's leg will be kicked or cut by the cleats on the bottom of the shoe. A major-foul.

HALFBACKS, MIDFIELDERS, LINKMEN: Players stationed in the middle of a team's formation, between the fullbacks and the forwards. See **Formation**.

HALF-TIME: The rest period, usually 5 minutes, between the two halves of a game.

HALF-VOLLEY, -PASS, -KICK: A pass or kick made just as the ball touches or rebounds from the ground. See **Volley**.

HALFWAY-FLAGS: Optional flags marking the midpoint of the touch-lines.

HALFWAY-LINE: A marked line running crosswise across the middle of the field from one touch-line to the other. See **Center-Line**.

HANDLING, HAND-BALL: A foul committed by intentionally touching the ball with the hands or arms. A major-foul.

HEADING: Striking the ball with the head.

HEAD-ON-TACKLE: To tackle by meeting the opponent head-on and blocking the ball with the feet. See **Tackle**.

HEELING: To kick or pass the ball backwards with the heel of the foot.

HIGH-KICKING: Kicking so high that it is dangerous to other players. See **Dangerous-Play**.

HITCH-KICK: See **Bicycle-Kick**.

HOLDING: Intentionally restraining an opponent by grasping with the hands or entangling with the arms. A major-foul.

HOOKING: To tackle by inserting a greatly extended leg from the side. See **Tackle**.

"HUNGARIAN OFFSIDE": See **Offside-Trap**.

INDIRECT-FREE-KICK: A free-kick that may not score unless it is touched by a second player from either team after the initial kick. See **Free-Kick**, **Direct-Free-Kick**.

INJURY-TIME: Extra time added to the length of a game by the referee to compensate for time lost caring for injured players.

INSIDE- OF- THE- FOOT- PASS: See Push-Pass.

INSIDE- OF- THE- FOOT- TRAP: See Receiving.

INSIDES, INSIDE- FORWARDS: Forwards stationed near the center line of the field. See **Forwards**.

INSTEP, INSTEP- PASS, - DRIVE: The upper side of the foot, between the toes and the ankle. A pass or drive made with the instep.

INSWINGER- BALL: A corner-kick made with a spin that causes it to curve toward the mouth of the goal, creating a direct scoring opportunity. See **Bending-The-Ball**.

INTENTIONAL- FOUL: A foul committed with foreknowledge, but with intention to play the ball. May be penalized with a free-kick. See **Accidental-Foul, Deliberate-Foul**.

IN- TOUCH: Out-of-bounds over a touch-line of the playing field. See **Touch, Touch-Lines**.

JAVELIN- THROW: A one-handed throw by the goal-keeper. See **Throw**.

JERSEY: A shirt with a player's number on it worn as part of the uniform.

JUMPING- AT- AN- OPPONENT: Intentionally jumping into the air at an opponent in a manner that risks injurious contact. A major-foul.

KEEPER: See **Goal-Keeper**.

KICKING- AN- OPPONENT: Intentionally kicking an opponent rather than the ball. A major-foul.

"KICKING- TO- THE- KEEPER" : A term used here to describe a prohibited time-wasting maneuver in which a player kicks the ball to his own goal-keeper, who catches it with the hands, and releases it back to a team-mate.

KICK- OFF: The taking of the initial kick to begin or restart play. The kick itself is referred to as a "place-kick." Here, the term "kick-off" refers to both the kick and the taking of the kick at the beginning of the game, to begin the second half, to begin any overtime periods, and to restart play after a goal has been scored. See **Place-Kick**.

KICKS- FROM- THE- PENALTY- KICK- MARK: A method of deciding the winner in a tied game.

"LAW 18": An unwritten convention in soccer that gives referees the authority to interpret the official rules according to common sense, and to make decisions on the spot in cases not covered by the written rules. See "Laws Of The Game."

"LAWS OF THE GAME" : The official rules of the game, promulgated by the international governing body, the Fédération Internationale de Football Association (FIFA) in Zurich, Switzerland. There are 17 Laws covering the various aspects of play. See **Law 18**.

LEAD- PASS: To pass the ball ahead of a teammate so that it may be received without breaking stride.

LEG- TRAPPING: See Receiving.

LINESMEN: Assistants to the referee stationed along the touch-lines during a match. They assume varying degrees of authority, depending on the officiating system used and the wishes of the referee. See **Club-Linesmen, Neutral-Linesmen**.

LINKMEN: See Halfbacks.

LOFT, LOFT- PASS, LOFTED- DRIVE: A kick made high into the air over the heads of opponents.

MAJOR-FOULS, PENAL-FOULS: A group of 9 specific fouls which are penalized by the awarding of direct-free-kicks or penalty-kicks to the fouled team. See **Minor-Fouls**.

MARKING, MARKING-MAN-TO-MAN, ONE-ON-ONE-DEFENSE: A defensive tactic in which defenders are assigned individual opponents whom they guard very closely. See **Zone Defense**.

MIDFIELDERS: See **Halfbacks**.

MINOR-FOULS, NON-PENAL-FOULS: Fouls penalized by the awarding of indirect-free-kicks to the fouled team. See **Major-Foul**.

MISCONDUCT: Violations against the spirit of the game, such as time wasting or ungentlemanly conduct. Penalized with cautions or ejections. See **Cautions, Ejections, Fouls**.

NARROWING-THE-ANGLE: See **Advancing-From-The-Goal**.

NEAR-POST: Whichever goal-post is nearest the ball at any particular moment of play. See **Far-Post**.

NEAR-POST-CROSS: A pass made toward the goal-post nearest the kicker. See **Far-Post-Cross**.

NEUTRAL-LINESMEN: Trained assistants to the referee stationed along the touch-lines during a match. They assist in signalling calls. See **Linesmen, Club-Linesmen**.

NON-PENAL-FOUL: See **Minor-Foul**.

OBSTRUCTION: Intentionally blocking an opponent's path, with the primary object not being to play the ball. Also, attempting to prevent a goal-keeper from releasing the ball back into play after he has gained possession of it with his hands. A Minor-Foul. See **Screening**.

OFFENSE, ATTACK: The team having possession of the ball.

OFFSIDE, OFFSIDE-RULE: An offensive violation which may be called when attacking players position themselves ahead of the ball. Also, the rule defining this violation. Subject to many conditions and exemptions.

OFFSIDE-TRAP, "HUNGARIAN OFFSIDE": A legal tactic in which defenders suddenly move forward in unison in an attempt to catch an attacking player in an offside position, thus neutralizing the attack and drawing an indirect-free-kick.

ONE-ON-ONE-DEFENSE: See **Marking**.

ONE-TOUCH-PASS, -PLAY: To send the ball away with a single touch of the foot or body, without maintaining control over it. See **Two-Touch-Pass**.

OUT-OF-BOUNDS: A dead-ball condition that occurs when the entire ball passes completely beyond one of the boundary lines of the field.

OUTSIDE-OF-THE-FOOT-PASS: To pass by kicking the ball with the outside of the foot. Usually puts spin on the ball, sending it on a curving path.

OUTSIDE-OF-THE-FOOT-TRAP: See **Receiving**.

OUTSIDES, OUTSIDE-FORWARDS: See **Wingers**.

OUTSWINGER-BALL: A corner-kick made with a spin that causes it to curve away from the goal, creating an indirect scoring opportunity as the kicker's teammates come in to attack. See **Bending-The-Ball**.

OVERARM-THROW: A one-handed throw by the goal-keeper. See **Throw**.

OVERHEAD-VOLLEY: See **Bicycle-Kick**.

OVERLAP-RUN: To run without the ball to a position in front of one's teammates. See **Running-Off-The-Ball**.

OVER- THE- BALL: See **Going-Over-The-Ball**.

PASS: To kick the ball to a teammate.

PENAL- FOULS: See **Major-Fouls**.

PENALTY- ARCS: The semi-circular lines of 10-yard radius located just outside the penalty areas.

PENALTY- AREAS, - BOXES: The marked 18 by 44-yard rectangular areas that surround the goal-areas. Penalty-areas include the goal-areas within them. Goal-keepers may handle the ball within their penalty-areas. A penalty-kick is awarded to the opposing team if a player commits one of the 9 major-fouls within his own penalty-area.

PENALTY- BOXES: See **Penalty-Areas**.

PENALTY- KICK: A special kick awarded to the opposing team when a player commits one of the 9 major-fouls inside his own penalty-area. Severe restrictions apply to the defense of penalty-kicks.

PENALTY- KICK- MARKS, PENALTY- SPOTS: The 9-inch diameter, marked points located 12 yards out from the centers of the goals. Penalty-kicks are taken from the penalty-kick-marks.

PIGEON- HOLES: Slang for the two extreme upper corners of the goals. Hard shots directly into the pigeon-holes are very difficult for the goal-keeper to stop.

PITCH: See **Field-Of-Play**.

PLACE- KICK: A kick made after the ball has been placed stationary on the center-mark. See **Kick-Off**.

PLACING- HANDS- ON- AN- OPPONENT: Intentionally touching an opponent. Same as holding, a major-foul.

PLAYING FIELD: See **Field-Of-Play**.

" PLAY ON! " OR "ADVANTAGE! PLAY ON! ": The command called out by the referee when he has chosen to acknowledge a foul but let play continue without interruption. See **Advantage-Rule**.

POKE- TACKLE: To tackle by inserting a foot and kicking the ball with the toes. See **Tackle**.

PROFESSIONAL FOUL: A deliberate foul committed to neutralize an obvious scoring opportunity. Penalized as serious foul play, a major-misconduct violation.

" PSEUDO- MINOR- FOUL" : A term used here to describe a technical violation of the rules which is treated similarly to a minor-foul, *i.e.,* an indirect-free-kick is given to the opposing team. Includes offside, goal-keeper violations, double-play, and misconduct whistles. See individual sections.

PUNCHING: See **Boxing**.

PUSHING- AN- OPPONENT: Intentionally pushing an opponent with the hands or arms. A major-foul.

PUSH- PASS, INSIDE- OF- THE- FOOT- PASS: The most common pass, made by kicking the ball with the inside of the foot.

QUARTER- CIRCLES: See **Corner-Areas**.

QUICK- FREE- KICK: A legal free-kick taken before defenders have moved back the required 10 yard distance. Taken in an attempt to catch the defense off guard.

RECEIVING, COLLECTING, TRAPPING: Gaining possession of a moving ball by absorbing its impact with some part of the body. The actual method of contact is called a "trap," which is named for the part of the body used. Thus, the ball may be received or collected with a chest-trap, shin-trap, stomach-trap, leg-trap, sole-of-the-foot-trap, inside-of-the-foot-trap, outside-of-the-foot-trap, thigh-trap, etc.

RED-CARD: A card displayed by the referee to signify that someone has been ejected from a game. See **Ejection**.

REDIRECTING: Changing the path of a moving ball by deflecting it with the foot or another part of the body.

REFEREE: The official responsible for controlling the game.

RELEASE: See **Distribution**.

RUNNING-OFF-THE-BALL: The movement of an attacking player without the ball into a favorable position to receive a pass or score a goal. See **Overlap-Run**.

SANDWICHING: A foul committed when two or more teammates converge to pin an opponent in place. A form of holding, a major-foul.

SAVE: The stopping or deflecting by the goal-keeper of a shot that would have otherwise scored a goal.

SCISSORS-KICK: See **Bicycle-Kick**.

SCREENING, SHIELDING: The legal positioning of the body between an opponent and a ball within playing distance. The primary intention must be to play the ball itself, and not to block the opponent. See **Obstruction**.

SCREW: See **Spin**.

SEND-OFF: See **Ejection**.

SHIELDING: See **Screening**.

SHIN-TRAPPING: See **Receiving**.

SHOOT, SHOT: To kick the ball directly at the goal.

SHOOT-OUT: A method of deciding the winner of a tied game.

SHOULDER-CHARGING: See **Fair-Charging**.

SIDEARM-THROW: A one-handed throw by the goal-keeper. See **Throw**.

SIX-YARD-LINES: The lines marking the edges of the goal-areas nearest the middle of the field. These lines are six yards from the goal-lines.

SLIDE-TACKLE: To tackle by kicking the ball away while sliding to the ground. See **Tackle**.

SOLE-OF-THE-FOOT-PASS: To pass by placing the foot on the ball and pulling it backwards.

SOLE-OF-THE-FOOT-TRAP: See **Receiving**.

SPIN, SCREW, ENGLISH: A spin applied to the ball which causes it to travel in a curving path.

SQUARE-PASS: A lateral pass that goes straight across the field.

STOMACH-TRAPPING: See **Receiving**.

STRIKING-AN-OPPONENT: Intentionally hitting an opponent. Also, spitting or throwing the ball or another object at an opponent. A major-foul.

STRIKERS, CENTER-FORWARDS: Attacking players stationed in the middle of a team's front line.

SUBSTITUTION: To replace a player on the field with one who has been waiting on the bench.

SUPPORT: An attacking player properly positioned to receive a pass from a teammate who has the ball. See **Cover**.

SWEEPER, SWEEPER-BACK: A fullback not assigned to man-to-man coverage who provides cover for other defenders in case they are beaten by an attacker. The last line of defense before the goal-keeper.

TACKLE: To legally challenge an opponent for control of the ball by inserting the foot and attempting to block the ball or kick the ball away.

TAKE-OVER-PASS, -PLAY: An attacking maneuver in which two teammates exchange the ball as they cross paths.

THIGH-TRAP: See **Receiving**.

THIRDS-OF-THE-FIELD: Transverse sections of the playing field designated as the "defending," "middle" and "attacking" thirds.

THROW: To put the ball back into play by throwing it with the hands. A goal-keeper is permitted to make two-handed throws, or one-handed base-ball-throws, javelin-throws, over-arm-throws, or sidearm-throws. All other players must throw two-handed, during throw-ins only. See **Throw-In**.

THROW-IN: A two-handed, overhead throw to put the ball back into play after it has gone out-of-bounds over a touch-line.

TOUCH: The out-of-bounds areas just outside the touch-lines or sidelines of the playing field. See **In-Touch, Touch-Lines**.

TOUCH-LINES: The lines marking the side boundaries of the field. The touch-lines are considered part of the field. See **In-Touch, Touch**.

TRAPPING: See **Receiving**.

TRIPPING-AN-OPPONENT: Intentionally causing an opponent to fall by blocking or entangling the legs. A major-foul.

TURNING-AN-OPPONENT: Causing a defensive player to turn toward his own goal to chase the ball or an attacking player.

TURNING-WITH-THE-BALL: To take control of a ball while facing one's own goal and move it towards the opponent's goal.

TWO-TOUCH-PASS, -PLAY: To send the ball away with two quick touches of the foot or body, while maintaining only the briefest control over it. See **One-Touch-Pass**.

VIOLENT-CHARGING: Intentionally violent bumping of an opponent, especially with a swing of the arm. A major-foul.

VOLLEY, FULL-VOLLEY, -PASS, -KICK: A kick or pass made while the ball is still in the air. See **Half-Volley**.

WALL: A defensive formation used during free-kicks, in which defending players stand side-by-side to form a "human wall" in front of their goal.

WALL-PASS: A special type of give-and-go pass made by kicking the ball to a teammate and then running forward. The teammate immediately returns the ball back to the first player as though it has reflected off a wall.

WINGERS, WINGS, OUTSIDES, OUTSIDE-FORWARDS: Forwards who play along the sidelines of the field. See **Forwards**.

WING-HALFBACKS: Halfbacks stationed along the sidelines of the field. See **Halfbacks**.

YELLOW-CARD: A card displayed by the referee to signify that a player has received a formal caution. See **Caution**.

ZONE-DEFENSE: A defensive strategy which assigns defenders responsibility for areas or "zones" of the field, rather than for specific opponents. See **Marking, Balance-In-Defense**.

Resources

Soccer rule books for the amateur adult, youth, high school and collegiate levels are adaptations of the official FIFA rules as promulgated by the Fédération Internationale de Football Association, and published in the United States by the U.S. Soccer Federation (USSF).

For youth soccer, local leagues are authorized by the U.S. Youth Soccer Association, a division of the USSF, to make minor alterations to the official FIFA rules according to their individual needs.

Youth soccer leagues sometimes make their rule changes available as pamphlets or informal photocopied information sheets.

Soccer rule books may also be obtained from the following sources:

Fédération Internationale de Football Association (FIFA), FIFA House, Hitzigweg 11, 8030 Zurich, Switzerland, Telephone 41-1/384-9595.

United States Soccer Federation (USSF), 1801-1811 S. Prairie Ave., Chicago, IL 60616. (312) 808-1300.

National Collegiate Athletic Association, 6201 College Blvd., Overland Park, KS 66211. (913) 339-1906.

Amateur Athletic Union, P.O. Box 68207, Indianapolis, IN 46268. (317) 872-2900.

Index

Notes

Can't find this book in the stores?

You may order your copy of Understanding Soccer directly from the publisher for $9.95, plus $3.00 for shipping by U.S. Mail Fourth Class Book Rate. (For orders of more than one book, add 50 cents shipping for each additional book.)

Please send me _____ copies of Understanding Soccer @ $9.95 .... _____

California residents please add $.89 sales tax per book .... _____

Shipping: Add $3.00 for first book, plus 50 cents per additional book ...... _____

(For U.S. Priority Mail, please add an additional $3.00) .... _____

Total _____

Name: _____

Address: _____

City/State/Zip: _____

Please send check or money order to: **Apples & Oranges, Inc.**
Attn: Book Orders
P.O. Box 2296K
Valley Center, CA 92082

For more information, please call (619) 751-8868, Fax (619) 751-8866